Mothering, Community, and Friendship

Edited by Dannabang Kuwabong,
Dorsía Smith Silva, and Essah Diaz

Mothering, Community, and Friendship
Edited by Dannabang Kuwabong, Dorsía Smith Silva, Essah Diaz

Copyright © 2022 Demeter Press

Individual copyright to their work is retained by the authors. All rights reserved. No part of this book may be reproduced or transmitted in any form by any means without permission in writing from the publisher.

Demeter Press
PO Box 197
Coe Hill, Ontario
Canada
K0L 1P0
Tel: 289-383-0134
Email: info@demeterpress.org
Website: www.demeterpress.org

Demeter Press logo based on the sculpture "Demeter" by Maria-Luise Bodirsky www.keramik-atelier.bodirsky.de

Printed and Bound in Canada

Cover design and typesetting: Michelle Pirovich
Proof reading: Jena Woodhouse

Library and Archives Canada Cataloguing in Publication
Title: Mothering, community, and friendship / edited by Dannabang Kuwabong, Dorsía Smith Silva, and Essah Díaz.
Names: Kuwabong, Dannabang, 1955- editor. | Silva, Dorsía Smith, editor. | Díaz, Essah, editor.
Description: Includes bibliographical references.
Identifiers: Canadiana 20210363576 | ISBN 9781772583748 (softcover)
Subjects: LCSH: Female friendship. | LCSH: Friendship. | LCSH: Motherhood. | LCSH: Mothers. | LCSH: Communities. | LCSH: Mothers—Social life and customs.
Classification: LCC HM1161 .M68 2022 | DDC 302.34085/2—dc23

Acknowledgments

The editors of this anthology wish to acknowledge the support of the Department of English–College of Humanities and the Department of English, College of General Studies, University of Puerto Rico, Rio Piedras Campus, as well as Dr. Andrea O'Reilly, without whose great patience, understanding, and encouragement this project would never have come to completion. We also wish to express our sincerest appreciation to Dr. Janet MacLennan of the Department of English, College of Humanities, University of Puerto Rico, Rio Piedras, and Dr. Norma I. Rivera, Graduate School of Planning, University of Puerto Rico, Rio Piedras for their initial input that helped shape the book. Finally, we wish to thank all of the contributors that dedicated their time and made this book possible. We send our heartfelt sympathy to the family and friends of contributor, Hannah Swamidoss, who passed away before the publication of this book.

Contents

Acknowledgments
3

Introduction: Fluid Communities, Illusive Friendships, Phenomenal Mothering
Dannabang Kuwabong, Dorsía Smith Silva, and Essah Diaz
9

I. Motherhood and Communities
21

1.
Hiccups and Highlights of Academic Motherhood:
Three Accounts of Cultivating Community and Friendship
as an Academic and a Mom
Mary King, Skye Chernichky-Karcher, and Jessica Pauly
23

2.
Finding Community as a Mother and a Scholar
Nicole L. Willey
41

3.
Mothers, Mentors, and Communities in Alice Walker's
The Color Purple and Sapphire's *Push*
Zsuzsanna Lénárt Muszka
53

4.
The Ripple Effect of Mothering in a Global Community:
From Bloomington to Bogotá
Silvia Rivera-Largacha and Angela N. Castañeda
69

5.
Film as Invitational Rhetoric:
Transcending Motherhood Narratives through Community
in *20th Century Women*
Rachel D. Davidson and Catherine A. Dobris
85

6.
Mma Habiba:
Maternal Outcast or Community Mother
Dannabang Kuwabong
109

7.
Maria's Maternal Rage against the Community
Dannabang Kuwabong
115

8.
Fifty-Five Miles
Heather Robinson
119

II. Motherhood and Friendship
123

9.
Supportive and Destructive Female Relationships
in Mariama Bâ's *So Long a Letter*
Sherean Shehada
125

10.
"Can We All Stand Together and Agree on This?" Space, Place, and Mothering in Lauren Mills's *Minna's Patchwork Coat*
Hannah Swamidoss
141

11.
Chinese Mothers Creating a Community of Maternal Support
Catherine Ma
153

12.
Beyond DNA
Janice Tuck Lively and Mary Barbara Walsh
167

13.
A "Community of Comothers": How Friendships with Expatriate Mothers Create Intercultural Understanding
Meredith Stephens
185

Notes on Contributors
199

Introduction

Fluid Communities, Illusive Friendships, Phenomenal Mothering

Dannabang Kuwabong, Dorsía Smith Silva, and Essah Diaz

Without community there is no liberation, only the most vulnerable and temporary armistice between an individual and her oppression.

—Audre Lorde 112

Mothering, Community, and Friendship offers a unique trans-, cross-, and interdisciplinary contribution to the divergent, complex experiences of motherhood and mothering in contemporary multiform, assiduous or exiguous communities, and friendships. Using a feminist lens, this book integrates the disciplines of literary criticism, trauma and narrative witnessing, media studies, children's literature, diaspora studies, cultural analysis, and poetry to weave a rich multifaceted quilt of knowledge on mothering. Authors reflect on individual and collective journeys that ultimately lead to understanding, celebrating, lamenting, and mapping their mothering journeys. As authors recall their experiences as academics, artists, activists, educators, and members of communities from different spaces in time, we come to understand that the realities of mothering are sometimes indescribable. This book is a response to MIRCI's call for trans-, cross-, and interdisciplinary approaches that interrogate, challenge, affirm, demystify, decolonize, and refine notions of mothering.

J.S. Savage argues that "Women have passed down their stories of wisdom and confidence in their ability to birth until the modern era" (8). Hence, all cultures historically have recognized birthing and mothering as women's work supported by women's knowing (8). In her essay "Community Mothering: The Relationship Between Mothering and The Community Work of Black Women," Edwards discusses the role of community in African American mothering praxes and connects their unique practice of mothering based on friendship, community, and cultural genealogy traceable back to West Africa and the history of slavery and segregation.

Many mothers find it difficult to find a supportive community of friends, or supportive family members, in their mothering journey, which can make mothering a lonely experience. Mothers are deprived of the lessons on mothering from other mothers. Stories, such as those shared in this collection, offer psychological and emotional support in the task of mothering. Networks of family, friends, and community create safe spaces for expectant mothers—be they first-time mothers, or experienced mothers—to interact face to face, or virtually, and share their concerns, joys, and expectations as well as give and receive advice about pregnancy, birth, childcare, etc. (Drentea and Moren-Cross). In addition to experiential knowledge, communities of friends and family offer warmth, love, and encouragement that may differ from the professional advice offered by professional midwives, nurses, and doctors, which may solely focus on science-based studies (Drentea and Moren-Cross; Alsarve; Arendell).

This collection brings together views and experiences that intentionally intertwine to show the interrelatedness of mothering, community, and friendship and contributes to the growing importance of friendship and community to healthy mothering and motherhood. Building on Jenny Alsarve's research, "One can assume that relationships with friends (in addition to kin relationships) are especially important for lone mothers. These relationships can offer for instance emotional and practical support, a support that can be imperative for lone mothers" (402). Friendship is tied to the idea of community—to an inner type of circle that provides more intimate emotional, practical, and psychological support to a mother. A community of mothers and friends form a support network, not only for the mother but also for the children (412). Community is not just a grouping of people in a confined geographical space. A community in mothering praxes is "a strong attachment that [mothers] feel toward others [mothers] based on where they live, work, or go to school, or with which groups they affiliate" (Anderson and Milligan 32). Thus, in mothering practices, to assert that one belongs to a community is to stress a feeling of emotional, social, and cultural affinity and commitment to the ideals of the group as "spatially or nonspatially defined" (Anderson and Milligan 32).

Andrea Anderson and Sharon Milligan suggest four components to sustain community—"membership, influence, integration, and fulfillment of needs"—which they assert "can be readily applied to a variety of geographically bound and interest-oriented communities" used in this collection (34). They demonstrate that fostering a sense of unity "taps into community members' underlying feelings of belonging, togetherness, mutuality, and camaraderie that are theoretically linked to behaviors that enhance community life" (32). A community in mothering implies, therefore, the possession of a unique psychological, emotional, social, and experiential sentiment that "captures how much [mothers] stick together or feel like members" (Anderson and Milligan 32-34) of a mothering group to which they contribute and from which they benefit in many tangible and nontangible ways. Generally, Anderson and Milligan advocate that sense of "community is a feeling that members have of belonging and being important to each other, and a shared faith that members' needs will be met by their commitment to be together" (34).

Mothering, Community, and Friendship addresses how some mothers find strength in their communities and friendships, whereas others discuss their struggles with loneliness and emotional pain due to their lack of community and friendship. As a collection, these chapters reflect the impossibility of representing mothering, community, and friendship from a monolithic perspective; they refute idealized assumptions about motherhood and reveal underlying anxieties of the many who negotiate motherhood and a career. Each chapter articulates these tricky and sometimes irreconcilable positions to explore the myriad possibilities and problems of mothering.

Role of Community and Mothering

How we experience and engage with friendship and community is evolving and varies from culture to culture. In 2003, Rosemarie Rizzo Parse identified a shift in the understanding of community: "Scholars in the human sciences are turning attention to the community as more than a location or group with similar interests" (xi). She continued: "Community is also concerned with meaning [as well as narratives that] comprise meaning moments chosen by community members as they communicate their perceptions of themselves to others within and without the community. Community comes about with communication, which is the process of sharing experiences" (2). Therefore, "sharing experiences is fundamental to the community" (2). Being a part of a community is important when beginning to mother. Some experiences of mothering are not perfect; therefore, it is important to connect with others who encourage or identify with similar struggles.

A community is a place where one feels most at home. The authors in this collection show how their lives evolved as their communities were created over time, and how in various spaces, they were embraced by a community that has encouraged them throughout their mothering journey. Communities can be found online, through mutual friends, or sometimes through work (Gattoni 2013).

Role of Friendship and Mothering

Recent studies on friendship among pregnant women and new mothers helped to "suggest that friendships made at antenatal classes are not unique but also support women's mental health and enhance self-efficacy because the women give and gain reassurance that their babies are developing normally" (Nolan et al. 179). Their information shows how "[f]riendship reduces the risk of depression" and enhances the overall "well-being and happiness across the transition to motherhood" and "safeguards the mental, physical, and social health of babies who are adversely affected by unhappy and unresponsive mothers" (Nolan et al. 179). New mothers in the group affirmed they "needed opportunities [among friends] to reassure themselves that their mothering was on a par with that of other women and that their babies were developing normally" (Nolan et al. 181).

Maria Lugones and Pat Alake Rosezelle define friendship as a "kind of practical love that commits one to perceptual changes in the knowledge of other persons" (141), one that thrives on flexibility. Rules of engagement are constantly negotiable. A friendship between women is driven by "the varied realities, world, of women," and hence "friendship must be conceived along plural" interactive multivocal ways determined by practical love (143)—the vision of a true egalitarian feminist community.

Likewise, in a series of studies done among white mothers mothering their mixed-racial children, Vicki Harman discovered that these mothers felt compelled to "enlarge these networks, ... through support groups, friendships with people from minority ethnic backgrounds, and other interracial families" (1323) to combat the racism that curtailed their parenting circles. The bonding and practical love enabled these mothers to preserve their sanity and that of their mixed-race children. Friendship was vital to the physical, emotional, and mental wellbeing of mothers in addition to empowerment. Andrea O'Reilly argues that empowered mothering "begins with the recognition that both mothers and children benefit when the mother lives her life and practices mothering from a position of agency, authority, and autonomy" (190). In this regard, mothers feel empowered through meaningful friendships and the support systems they provide.

bell hooks stresses the ethic of love as the driver of true friendship—a "will to extend one's self for the purpose of nurturing one's own or another's spiritual growth" (6). Friendship, like love, by implication, is enduring human warmth towards another, and that warmth emanates from what Rebecca Bromwich and colleagues classify as related to "kindness, munificence, and commitment as well as closely connected" (9) to the principle of caring and nurturing. The authors continue: "Friendship is a fluid and not generally fixed relationship, which is based on affinity, as opposed to status, although there can be status-based friendships" (9). Resultantly, friendship can both be transitory or permanent depending on several extenuating and personal circumstances in the lives of the friends.

In *Girlfriends and Post-feminist Sisterhood*, Alison Winch criticizes contemporary women's friendship as neoliberal competitive self-branding posturing as "postfeminist sisterhood" and predetermined by Anglo-American white "liberal feminist rhetoric of agency and choice"

(2). Friendship no longer is understood as a necessary and deliberate love endeavour. It has become a ritualized self-serving drive dependent on receiving from others without giving to others. Winch details how this neoliberal competitiveness among women generates feelings of guilt, shame, and despair in women by presenting them with the false choice between mothering and career advancement.

Count on Me: Tales of Sisterhoods and Fierce Friendships, edited by Adriana López, offers a more soothing collection of individual narratives and reflections. Nora de Hoyes writes that women's relationships are unique: "Reaching out to friends is a woman's natural response to stress. It said these friendships can bring us peace, fill the emotional shortcomings in our romantic relationships, and help us remember what lies deep inside every one of us. Women are a source of strength to each other" (ix). Friendship and community serve as sites of cooperative mentoring, interdependence, and collective group empowerment.

Overview of *Mothering, Community, and Friendship*

Motherhood, Community, and Friendship quilts together many voices and passions while exploring issues of friendship. In "Hiccups and Highlights of Academic Motherhood: Three Accounts of Cultivating Community and Friendship as an Academic and a Mom," Mary King, a mother and tenured professor, Skye Chernichky-Karcher, a mother transitioning into a tenure-track job, and Jessica Pauly, a mother and graduate student, narrate their individual yet intersecting experiences in their struggles to find a balance between mothering and career aspirations, showing how friendship among them has been the bedrock of their success.

Nicole L. Willey's "Finding Community as a Mother and a Scholar" reflects on how she found friendship and community. Willey discusses how friendships became harder to find as she grew older and presents how a community of friends with a passion for reading became her refuge. Discussing how early rejections by academia traumatized her, she praises MIRCI (formerly ARM) and Demeter Press for providing the platform and community in which she has grown both as a mother and an academic.

In "Mothers, Mentors, and Communities in Alice Walker's *The Color Purple* and Sapphire's *Push*," Zsuzsanna Lénárt-Muszka discusses the influence of communities and friendships on mothers and motherhood. She reveals that the protagonists in both books suffer multiple cases of abuse engineered through systemic patriarchy: emotional and physical. They both lose custody of their children but ultimately rediscover their roles as mothers through the assistance of a community of female friends and mentors.

Silvia Rivera Largacha and Angela N. Castañeda's "The Ripple Effect of Mothering in a Global Community: From Bloomington to Bogotá" explores the role friendship plays in connecting and impacting distant mothering communities. The authors follow the effects of mothering through various communities in Bloomington, Indiana to Bogotá, Colombia. Using autoethnography, they examine the multiple intersections of mothering cross-culturally. They assert that this study has fostered friendships and nurtured global cooperative community support networks of mothers that empower women.

In "Film as Invitational Rhetoric: Transcending Motherhood Narratives through Community in *20th Century Women*," Rachel D. Davidson and Catherine A. Dobris assert that *20th Century Women* presents mothering as empowering through community and friendship. A community of friends helps Dorthea Fields, a mother, in raising her teenage son, Jamie, in "cooperative, non-adversarial, and ethical communication" ways (Foss and Griffin 15). Thus, the movie shows how mothering, community, and friendship can be empowering to women.

Dannabang Kuwabong concludes the motherhood and communities' section with two poems: "Mma Habiba: Maternal Outcast or Community Mothering" and "Maria's Maternal Rage against the Community." The first poem is inspired by the life of a mysterious woman who, though an outcast in the village, is nonetheless a community mother. Irma and Maria are symbolized as "the womb that nourished our spirits" and as metaphors for Mary in the Catholic Church and "that spilled innocent blood" by Herod.

In the poem "Fifty-Five Miles," Heather Robinson takes the reader on a journey of finding a community as a white, lesbian, academic mother. Each stanza details the experiences she goes through while breastfeeding her daughter. The use of alliteration and imagery demonstrates the day-to-day life of a modern mum. She takes us on her journey to find a community of alike women while balancing a full-time job.

Sherean Shehada in "Supportive and Destructive Female Relationships in Mariama Bâ's *So Long a Letter*" explores how friendship and community help Ramatoulaye in Bâ's novella. Ramatoulaye's ability to deal with the trauma of being abandoned as wife and mother is grounded in Wolof ideals of motherhood, community, and friendship. Hader argues that these function as emotional, psychological, and social bonds that Wolof women create for both individual and group healing and empowerment.

In "'Can We All Stand Together and Agree on This?': Space, Place, and Mothering in Lauren Mills's *Minna's Patchwork Coat*," Hannah Swamidoss discusses the details of space and place as part of the fabric of a community. Through the textile arts, the public and domestic spheres of motherhood can be threaded together, especially when there is a community of friends willing to share stories and take risks to create a community.

In "Chinese Mothers Creating a Community of Maternal Support," Catherine Ma explores the development of several important maternal friendships in her life as she navigates motherhood through the lenses of an academic and a Chinese immigrant. Her chapter details the significance of friendships in immigration experiences, especially for Chinese mothers. Ma's writing also addresses the impact of the Chinese diaspora on community building, cultural differences in fostering friendships, and the protective health benefits of lasting friendships.

In "Beyond DNA," Janice Tuck Lively and Mary Barbara Walsh reflect on their personal experiences with their mothers. Their roundtable style discussion reveals the complications of mother-daughter and sibling relations that are often discussed in women's studies. Using their own experiences, Lively and Walsh take the reader on imaginary journeys across families, time, and space and open up possibilities for change in relationships between women.

In "A 'Community of Comothers': How Friendships with Expatriate Mothers Create Intercultural Understanding," Meredith Stephens explores friendships cross-culturally. Cultural differences affect how mothering and friendship are constructed. Contemporary women whose lives are intersected with cross-cultural living demands, she argues, need to develop intercultural literacy to facilitate their mothering practices cross-culturally, even as they seek to form communities of friends cross-culturally.

Conclusion

Mothering, Community and Friendship demonstrates the complexity of the meaning of community and friendship within spatially segregated, fluid, and highly mobile, individualized societies. Finding a community of friends takes time, endurance, and strength, as shown by the authors in this collection. The authors share their stories about mothering, community, and friendship, neither to romanticize these experiences nor to vilify them. For those who aspire to be mothers, who are mothers, or have retired from mothering, and for men too, this book is for you, your friends, and your community.

Works Cited

Alsarve, Jenny. "Friendship, Reciprocity, and Similarity: Lone Mothers and Their Relationships with Friends." *Community, Work & Family*, vol. 23, no. 4, 2019, pp. 401-418.

Anderson, Andrea A., and Sharon Milligan. "Social Capital and Community Building." *Aspen Institute Roundtable on Community Change. Community Change: Theories, Practice, and Evidence*, edited by Karen Fulbright-Anderson and Patricia Auspos, Aspen Institute, 2006, pp. 21-60.

Arendell, Teresa. "Conceiving and Investigating Motherhood: The Decade's Scholarship." *Journal of Marriage and the Family*, vol. 62, no. 4, 2000, pp. 1192-1207.

Barnes, Marian. *Care in Everyday Life: An Ethic of Care in Practice*. The Policy Press, 2012.

Bonois, Andrea. *The Friendship Fix: The Complete Guide to Choosing, Losing, and Keeping Up with Your Friends*. St. Martin's Griffin, 2011.

Bromwich, Rebecca, et al. "Introduction." *Critical Perspectives on 21st Century Friendship, Polyamory, Polygamy, and Platonic Affinity*, edited by Rebecca Bromwich, Olivia Ungar, and Noémi Richard, Demeter Press, 2019, pp. 7-12.

Büskens, Petra. "The Impossibility of 'Natural Parenting' for Modern Mothers: On Social Structure and the Formation of Habit." *Mother Matters: Motherhood as Discourse and Practice*, edited by Andrea O'Reilly. Demeter Press, 2001, pp. 98-110.

Drentea, Patricia, and Jennifer L. Moren-Cross. "Social Capital and Social Support on the Web: The Case of an Internet Mother Site." *Sociology of Health & Illness*, vol. 27, no. 7, 2005, pp. 920-43.

Drentea, Patricia, and Jennifer L. Moren-Cross. "Online Motherhood: A Com-munity of Mothers Revisited." *Motherhood Online*, edited by M. Moravec, Cambridge Scholars Publishing, 2011, pp. 47-59.

Edwards, Arlene E. "Community Mothering, The Relationship Between Mothering and The Community Work of Black Women." *JARM/JMI*, vol.2, no. 2, 2004, pp. 87-100.

Foss, Sonja K., and Cindy L. Griffin. "Beyond Persuasion: A Proposal for an Invitational Rhetoric." *Communication Monographs*, vol. 62, no. 1, 1995, pp. 2-18.

Gattoni, Alice Leigh. *Breaking the Silence: The Role of Online Community in the Transition to Motherhood*. PhD Dissertation. University of Wisconsin, Milwaukee, 2013.

Gardiner, Judith Kegan. "Women's Friendships, Feminist Friendships." *Feminist Studies*, vol. 42, no. 2, 2016, pp. 484-501.

Harman, Vicki. "Social Capital and the Informal Support Networks of Lone White Mothers of Mixed-Parentage Children." *Ethnic and Racial Studies*, vol. 36, no. 8, 2013, pp. 1323-41.

hooks, bell. *All About Love. New Visions*. Harper, 2000.

Kinser, Amber E. *Motherhood and Feminism*. Seal Press, 2010.

Lorde, Audre. *Sister Outsider: Essays and Speeches*. Crossing Press, 2007, pp. 110-114.

López, Adriana V. *Count on Me: Tales of Sisterhoods and Fierce Friendships*. Atria, 2012.

Lugones, Maria, and Pat Alake Rosezelle. "Sisterhood and Friendship as Feminist Models." *Feminism and Community*, edited by Penny A Weiss and Marilyn Friedman, Temple University Press, 1995, pp. 135-46.

Moravec, Michelle. "Expectant Motherhood: How Online Communities Shape Pregnancy." *Motherhood Online*, edited by Moravec. Cam-bridge Scholars Publishing, 2011, pp. 2-22.

Nolan, Mary L. et al. "Making friends at antenatal classes: a qualitative exploration of friendship across the transition to motherhood." *The*

Journal of Perinatal Education vol. 21, no. 3, 2012, pp. 178-185.

O'Reilly, Andrea. "Feminist Mothering." *Mothers, Mothering, and Motherhood Across Cultural Differences*, edited by Andrea O'Reilly, Demeter, 2014, pp. 183-205.

Parse, Rosemarie Rizzo. *Community: A Human Becoming Perspective.* Jones and Bartlett Pub., 2003.

Sandercock, Leonie, and Ann Forsyth. "A Gender Agenda: New Directions for Planning Theory." *Journal of the American Planning Association*, vol. 58, no. 1, 1992, pp. 49-59.

Savage, J. S. "Birth Stories: A Way of Knowing in Childbirth Education." *Journal of Perinatal Education*, vol. 10, no. 3, 2001, pp. 3-9.

Winch, Alison. *Girlfriends and Postfeminist Sisterhood*. Palgrave Macmillan, 2013.

I.
Motherhood and Communities

Chapter 1

Hiccups and Highlights of Academic Motherhood: Three Accounts of Cultivating Community and Friendship as an Academic and a Mom

Mary King, Skye Chernichky-Karcher, and Jessica Pauly

Scholars have recently focused more on work-life balance among professionals, especially for women. The literature often explores the complicated skills needed by women to enable them to navigate between competing demands in their professional careers and their domestic lives as mothers. Although the boundaries between working outside the home and mothering as a domestic responsibility have been narrowed by advances in technology, most women still find it difficult to blend their professional careers with the home space while simultaneously playing mothering roles (Fonner and Roloff 205-31; Leonardi et al. 85-105). This issue is especially salient for women who may want to progress in their academic careers without sacrificing their desire for motherhood. Research suggests that although women are graduating from universities at high rates, they are not as equally represented in academic positions (Harper et al. 237-57). Furthermore, academic mothers often fail to meet professional benchmarks (e.g., tenure and promotion) at the same rate as their male counterparts (Wolfinger et al. 388-405), resulting in associated psychoemotional stresses that dampen their abilities to meet their goals. Women academics also often report psychoemotional tensions between when to have children and how to manage work deadlines (Buzzanell and D'Enbeau 1199-1224; Townsley and Broadfoot 133-42), and the guilt they feel if choosing to have children negatively impacts meeting work deadlines or vice versa. Undoubtedly, it is the hope that the proliferation of virtual classrooms and online teaching technology, together with the online availability of material relevant for academic research and publication, may help women academics to make great strides in their work-related goals as well as to enjoy mothering roles all from home.

Based on the personal experiences of the three authors, this chapter addresses our experiences as academic mothers and how we tried to deal with our encounters with our communities and our friendships at three different stages of our academic trajectory. Jessica and Skye began their friendship and community in graduate school, where they were students together. It was during this time that Jessica gave birth to her first child. Skye became pregnant as she was transitioning from graduate school to her position as an assistant professor at a mid-sized state university. This is where she met Mary, who was also pregnant with her second son; their sons are only a month apart. Each of us had different experiences of pregnancy and childbirth, which gave rise to the collaboration on this chapter—first, as graduate students and as mothers; second, as new faculty and mothers transitioning into tenure-track positions, and third, as newly tenured professors and mothers. Each of us constructs personal narratives seeking to respond to three overarching themes: (1) our perceptions of mothering in academia before we became mothers and how these perceptions have changed; (2) our individual experiences of motherhood in the academic community; and (3) the role friendships play in the experience of mothering.

Mothering in Graduate School (Jessica Pauly)

From childhood, I had always wanted to be a mother even before I wanted a job in academia. Being a mother and having a family were non-negotiable for me. If I had to choose between being a career woman or a mother of a family, I would choose motherhood and family over career. The statement is indicative of my perspective of mothering in academia: defensive and uncertain. Before I became a mother, my perception of mothering in academia was easily condensed into one question: How?

When I began work on my master's degree, my husband and I had just married, and we were talking about starting a family. My advisor was encouraging. She suggested that graduate school was a good time to have a baby. I trusted her advice, since she had recently had two children of her own. Yet I had some doubts. When I checked for other examples of female academic mothers, the list was short. Moreover, my initial understandings of academic life (e.g., late nights writing papers and constantly taking on one too many research projects) did not seem to fit with my expectations of motherhood life (e.g., bedtime routines, random sick days, and doctor appointments). My assumptions were not comforted by stories I heard from colleagues about becoming a mother in graduate school. One particularly depressing story was shared by a colleague of mine. She knew a graduate student who informed her advisor she was pregnant, and her advisor's bitter response was simply: "What are you going to do about this?"

I was aware that academia requires a great amount of effort, foresight, time, and energy to advance and achieve tenure. This awareness was confirmed anecdotally from stories I heard from peers, colleagues, and professors. One of my biggest concerns was time. Time seemed to be both elusive and convicting. With so many tasks at various stages of completion at any given moment (e.g., research projects, grant proposals, and grading), weekends and holidays were rarely considered true time off but rather a time to catch up on things that had fallen to the wayside. Energy, too, was a necessity in academia. Without energy to manage multiple tasks and keep up with a bustling schedule, nothing would get done. I was baffled when I began to realize that adding mothering into the mix of academic life pressures would prove extremely difficult. Yet I was undeterred.

As I wrapped up my master's degree, I applied to PhD programs. I carefully considered who would be my primary advisor. Because I planned and hoped to have a baby, I wanted to know my advisor would be supportive of my desire to start a family. Although I was accepted to multiple programs, I chose to attend my graduate institution to work with my advisor who had a large family of her own. I often asked her how she did it. My advisor shared stories that made mothering as an academic sound simple, although I knew it could not possibly be the case. The more she told me, the more I wondered.

In the second year of my doctoral program, to my husband's and my sheer delight, I learned I was pregnant. I had nearly completed all coursework and was set to take my preliminary exams that fall; in retrospect, the timing could not have been better if we had planned it ourselves (we didn't!). I had a wonderful pregnancy, and my friends and academic community were excited for us and supportive. A group of friends from my graduate program even organized a baby shower for me and my husband, complete with snacks, tea, and multiple baby books as gifts. It was delightful to receive such special treatment as I approached a new chapter in life.

During the first few months of my baby's life, I was the only graduate student in my school to experience the unique life-changing experience of becoming a parent. Immediately after giving birth, I was encouraged to track my baby's eating, sleeping, and diaper changes. This required focused attention, and because I was sleep-deprived and exhausted most of the time, I spent a lot of energy tracking these daily activities. Naturally, a slower pace to life set in. I simply could not keep up with the same quick pace I had taken during life before the baby arrived; multitasking and hustling were not options. When the baby needed to eat, I had to stop what I was doing and sit down to breastfeed her. It was both humbling and life changing (not to mention one of my greatest joys during that period in my life). My colleagues were making strides in their academic careers and starting new research projects while I was simply trying to learn the ropes of being a mother. Slowly but surely, I learned that mothering requires greater focused attention, a slower pace to life, and a flexible schedule. At times I felt a little lonely, and sometimes even frustrated. The slower pace required a flexible schedule, and I quickly learned to adjust my expectations on making appointments on time or meeting a friend or colleague out.

While many of my friends and colleagues did not understand the new demands of my life, they made a great effort to try to understand, listen, and check in often. One of my most treasured memories, as a beautiful example of the support I received, is when my husband, baby, and I arrived home for the first time after our hospital stay. Upon entering our house, my dear graduate school friends had decorated our home with balloons, flowers, snacks, and a full fridge of food. It was a thoughtful and generous surprise, and I felt so loved and cared for.

I was relieved that despite the horror stories I had heard from other academic women, I did not have one negative interaction with anyone in my academic community during my pregnancy and postpartum experience. Even though the demands of academia and motherhood were drastically different and seemingly difficult to merge, they seemed to work out for me. In the weeks and months after giving birth to my daughter, I discovered that mothering as an academic just happens; my husband, daughter and I simply take one day at a time. We have found our new normal. I had expected mothering as an academic to be involved with difficult decision making, careful planning, and strong organizational skills. But what I realized was that there is less forethought than I had anticipated and more reactive flexibility at play. This meant that instead of anticipating my baby's schedule and planning around it, I spent more time letting my baby's schedule unfold as it needed and worked around opportunities for her needs. I learned that there is no time to think about how to do both academia and motherhood; I just do it. Mothering in academia, for me, is a chain of events and experiences that seem to work out despite the odds.

I would be remiss not to add that I understand I have a wonderful life partner, friends, and an academic community providing incredible love and support. The colleagues and friends I mentioned in this narrative were near and dear to my heart. They made their place in my life clear by informing me with both astute wisdom and generous spirit: "It takes a village. Know that we are in your village." I am fortunate to have found my village, and I have been able to make being a mother and academic work because of them.

Transitioning to Motherhood and the Tenure Track (Skye Chernichky-Karcher)

As a graduate student, "When is the 'right' time to start having children?" was a popular topic of conversation among the female students. Some claimed it was in your third year of graduate school; others said it was after graduation while on tenure track. Of course, when you asked those who had children, the answer was always "It's never the right time." During graduate school, my significant other and I were considering marriage and having serious conversations about what our future family would look like. It was early on that we decided we did want children, and the conversation turned to "When should we start trying?"

By this time almost all my college friends had children; many of them had more than one. I remember feeling like the sands of time were running out. If I was going to be a mother, we needed to start right away. I knew that I had fertility issues, and the question of whether we could get pregnant without medical intervention constantly weighed on my mind. Yet while the urge to start my family was strong, we waited. Perhaps this was because our lives were already so stressful between job responsibilities, prelims, and writing a dissertation. Or perhaps because financially, we didn't feel ready to expand our family. Whatever the reason, the answer was always "Let's wait until [insert next big benchmark]."

This theme of waiting for the right time embodies what my perception of mothering in academia was before I became a mother myself. And so perfectly nestled in this conversation of timing is a very important tension between work and family identities. What my friends, my significant other, and I so skillfully talked around was the tension between becoming the academics we all were working tirelessly to become or becoming mothers. Never did we discuss ways in which we could successfully be both.

This tension continues to embody my perceptions of motherhood in academia. I feel as though I make the choice, sometimes daily, whether I should prioritize my identity as a teacher-scholar or if I should devote my limited energy to being at home with my son. What often results is a poor combination of managing both identities and a feeling of never being truly successful at either job, which almost always results in feelings of guilt—guilt that I'm not being a good mother by spending enough time with my son or the guilt that I didn't get that manuscript out on time or I didn't finish grading because I was cuddling with my child and couldn't pull myself away. No matter the choice, it always seems to result in guilt about what is not getting accomplished.

Thankfully, I had the benefit of a supportive academic community. I accepted my current tenure-track position in mid-March and found out I was pregnant at the end of that same month. The news of our pregnancy was shocking. We were not actively trying, and I was told that we likely would not be able to get pregnant on our own. The news of our pregnancy also came as I worked tirelessly to finish my dissertation, find housing in a different state, and prepare to pack all of our belongings up to move. It felt like the entirety of April and May was spent trying to not be sick while simultaneously trying to do all of the things. I was on a dissertation fellowship during that time. When I received the fellowship, I reached out to a few colleagues (all women) who were also dissertating to start a writing group that met weekly. These women were the first in my academic community to learn I was pregnant. I was having a hard time focusing soon after we learned of the pregnancy, and I ended up just blurting it out in the middle of a writing session. I believe my colleagues, now friends, were both surprised and excited by my news. They immediately found ways to encourage and support my efforts to continue my academic activities while also encouraging me to engage in self-care.

One of the biggest challenges I faced as I prepared to transition from graduate student life to my new role as a tenure-track faculty member while pregnant was informing my new department chair that I would need to take maternity leave three-quarters of the way through my first semester. I had only met her once during my campus interview. Again, I felt incredibly guilty, as if I had done this terrible thing by getting pregnant just as I was beginning a new job. I was also unaware of the benefits available, as this wasn't one of my concerns when I interviewed for the position. I remember turning to the members of my writing group for advice on how to deliver the news. We discussed the benefits of calling versus writing an email. I wanted to pretend that it wasn't happening and avoid the situation, but they encouraged and supported me every step of the way.

In the end, I settled on an email that I agonized over for more than a week. My chair almost immediately called me on the phone. She communicated her congratulations and excitement for us while I apologized for this complication. She assured me that my courses would be covered and provided me with all of the relevant information for informing human resources. I remember being so relieved by her supportive response. I continued to feel supported as several faculty volunteered to take over my courses during my leave, two of my new colleagues (who also happened to be close friends) threw me the most wonderful baby shower, and my chair and senior faculty advised me on the best ways to balance my responsibilities as a new faculty member and as a new mother.

The support I received from both my academic community and from the network of other mothers and friends did not erase the tensions I had to deal with between my new identities as an academic and as an expectant mother. Transitioning from graduate school to a tenure-track position while also transitioning to motherhood comes with several challenges, many of which were mitigated by a strong academic community. As a new tenure-track faculty member, hired while still trying to complete my dissertation, I was very cautious when speaking about my pregnancy. I didn't want it to appear as though I was distracted or losing focus on completing my degree requirements, my teaching load, research, and other service requirements. Furthermore, among the cohort of five new faculty members with whom I was hired in my department, only one was a parent, which compelled me to downplay my status as an expectant mother and later as a mother after my son was born. I could build a strong interpersonal and collegial relationship, which in both the short and long term made life as a mother and an academic more bearable.

Undeniably, there were other challenges, such as relocation and finding a job for my spouse, that complicated the situation for me. My husband didn't find work right away, so he stayed in the town where we went to school, some six hundred miles away, and we lived apart until our son was born. It was incredibly difficult living in a new place in my third trimester, without my husband. Additionally, I had to find new healthcare providers, which was tough for me. I had lost the network of healthcare providers and friends I had grown attached to in my prior location. In our new location, I did not know many people and was not comfortable asking my new colleagues for the best place to have a baby. Eventually, things eased up as I settled down in my new job and built new bonds in the academic community while developing a personal network of friends in my new society where I would soon become a mother.

Mothering on the Other Side of Tenure (Mary King)

My perception of mothering in academia began in graduate school. As a graduate student, I saw a handful of my peers become mothers while completing their degrees. Aware that mothering is a challenge, in the toll it takes on one's patience and time, I thought becoming pregnant while in graduate school wasn't such a good thing, not because there was a rule of any sort but rather because it would delay obtaining my degree in good time. In graduate school, one is encouraged to work through the program quickly, obtain as much presence in the published world as possible, and get a job first before considering motherhood and related family responsibilities.

It is difficult to be successful in academia, and this point is true for graduate students as well as for established scholars. To achieve success, one must conduct research, present at conferences, and publish. For mothers, traveling for conferences can be difficult. As a pregnant woman, you are limited to traveling in your first two trimesters, and of course, once the child is born, there are additional considerations. For example, how soon after a child is born is it okay to leave for a conference? What about feeding the child? If you're breastfeeding, how much do you pump in anticipation of the conference? Are you able to bring expressed milk on an airplane? How much? Will there be a refrigerator in the hotel room? Will you have to pay an additional cost for a mini-fridge? These are all considerations mothers in academia face.

Additionally, the mentality of "publish or perish" is real, especially at research institutions. It is a challenge for all academics to prepare work for submission and publication. However, this challenge is especially salient for mothers. Sitting down to write a literature review or statistically analyze copious amounts of data is difficult when you have a hungry infant or a rambunctious two-year-old. Again, the time and commitment required for this process are challenging for anyone but especially for pregnant female academics and new mothers.

A benefit of academia is the ability to work from home. For me, this has always been an advantage—that is, until the birth of my children. I distinctly remember a time when my oldest was about one year old. He was playing in the living room, and I pulled out my laptop to get some work done. After a short time, I looked over and realized that even though we were in the same room, my child was alone. He was facing the wall, away from me, and playing by himself as I hammered away on a manuscript draft. This moment broke my heart. From then on, I made the commitment to work only when my children were not around. But this is a luxury I have as a tenured associate professor. Women on the tenure track are faced with the looming deadline of the tenure clock. Every day, every semester, that deadline races forwards, and there is constant pressure to work and produce. Even as a tenured professor, I feel pressure to keep it together, and I feel pressure to prove my children and personal life won't slow me down or interfere with my career. This is extremely difficult.

Mothering in academia is hard. There is still a bias against those who take time to have children and raise families. Academia is an ancient male-dominated institution, one that prides itself on liberal thinking and being at the forefront of our ever-changing society. However, when it comes to mothering, challenges, both pragmatic and social, remain. I've experienced some of these realities at negative moments in my academic career. A few years ago, I decided to apply for early promotion. Distasteful details aside, I was initially not supported by various individuals and experienced some pushback. A letter I received (as part of the application process) outlined the perceived deficiencies of my application and specifically highlighted that I was not recommended for promotion because I took maternity leave. Now, as many of us know no one can be denied promotion due to maternity leave (thanks to the Pregnancy Discrimination Act of 1978). I brought this to the attention of the committee who removed the line from the letter but did not alter their recommendation. In the end, despite the unsupportive letter, I was ranked second highest across the entire university based on my qualifications and was promoted.

Why is this story important? I had worked hard, done all of the things I was supposed to do, and even more. I knew I was in a good position for promotion, although this is never guaranteed. I thought if I didn't get promoted, it would be because I wasn't the best candidate, but I never thought I wouldn't be supported because I had taken maternity leave. In fact, in my mind, I was even more of an impressive candidate because I had achieved so much despite having taken maternity leave. The reality was that taking time to have a family was frowned upon.

Despite these challenges, I consider myself a successful academic and mother. However, this is largely in part because of my support network. I rely heavily on my family. I relocated out of state for my current job, and in so doing, I left my family approximately two hours away. I'm lucky. Many female academics move, often far distances, for their career. I drive only for two hours to see my family on any given weekend. Having our parents available to watch the children for a few hours here and there is an incredible source of support also. My relationship with my sister-in-law is also important to me. Our friendship is largely based on shared experiences. For example, our two oldest children are both boys, and we often share stories and advice on raising two little men. She's a great friend, and I feel I can be honest with her. I think our openness, sharing our strengths and struggles, is something that bonds.

The friendships I have with my academic peers are similar. The fact that my colleagues are my friends and my friends are my colleagues is helpful to me in many ways. From social support and sharing to tangible support when carrying a heavy workload, having colleagues as friends is a blessing. I know I won't feel judged for being honest if I'm struggling and need to talk or vent about anything, and I know there will be friends who will understand why that committee work wasn't done ahead of the deadline. It is a unique thing to have my friends as colleagues.

As great as it is to have my colleagues as friends, it can also be uncomfortable at times when talking about pregnancy and mothering. For example, I didn't expect my experiences of motherhood to start off feeling so weird. The process of telling my academic community of my pregnancy was strange. I remember feeling embarrassed when I told my chairperson (a supportive male, himself a father). Instead of feeling excited, it was almost this feeling of telling him, "I had sex!" Regardless, he was supportive of me and my pregnancy (and subsequent promotion woes, as previously noted).

Mothering in a post-tenure, academic job has its advantages. But the challenges to present at conferences and publish remain. I still feel as though I must make sure my colleagues know that my family is not interfering with my professional productivity and that seems somehow unfair. I'm not sure male professors feel this sense of obligation. As a tenured academic mother, I'm driven to "pay it forward" and be supportive of junior colleagues working so hard to be academic mothers because I know the challenges that they face are real and many.

Coffee with the Mothers: An Honest and Open Discussion

After we each reflected on our experiences of mothering in academia, we sat down and had a virtual coffee date. Our conversation was almost two hours long, and we highlighted the similarity of our experiences but also how mothering at different stages in academia is different. During our conversation, four themes emerged: control, guilt, embarrassment, and colliding worlds (friends, colleagues, and community).

Control

Control was a prominent theme that arose throughout our conversation. The conversation first turned to control as we discussed how we each planned our pregnancies for the right time. Jess recognized this:

> It just strikes me as humorous because for me and my husband, it took us a while ... some people are fortunate enough to say, "Okay, we're going to start growing our family now," and then it happens. But it's interesting that when you throw motherhood into the culture of academia, how much more it seems to be this control issue of timing and when is a good time and when is it a bad time and how it will affect your career and what perceptions your colleagues will have of you.

Skye echoed these sentiments as she reflected on her infertility challenges. Before becoming pregnant, she and her husband discussed with her doctor the medical interventions they would begin when they wanted to start their journey to parenthood, which resulted in seemingly too much control:

> But then I was given that control, and it was so much responsibility that it was crippling.... I was so mad. We were mad when we couldn't have a child when we wanted, but then ... we were mad because we had to schedule it. And some of that is linked to the challenges of infertility but also the tensions of motherhood and being a good academic.

Mary also reflected on her attempts to control the timing of her pregnancy:

> This isn't something I mentioned in my narrative, but it wasn't

easy for us either. We experienced loss.... We had two other pregnancies: one that didn't work out before Wes and one that didn't work out before Will. Those were the planned pregnancies. You know, we always planned "wouldn't it be nice to have a child in May?" I have three months to stay home and bond, but that didn't work out. Wes was born on the first day of school in the fall, and Will was born right at the end of the fall semester in December.

When discussing the root of this desire to control the timing of our pregnancies, we identified larger cultural misperceptions of our jobs in academia. We talked about how nonacademics have a perception that we are off in the summers and we have free time. As Skye mentioned: "The perception that people have of my job [is] that academia and being a teacher [are] family friendly. . . Having this "teacher" job, people are like, you have summers off and summer breaks and a flexible schedule, but they don't understand the demands of our job and how that conflicts with our ideas and our desires of the motherhood identity." Jess summarized our illusions of control and loss of control in academic motherhood: "It's funny how it still all comes back to control.... It's one of those things; people expect that you can control it.... This idea of control complicates the narrative of motherhood in academia."

Guilt

Guilt was another prominent theme across each of our narratives. We discussed the guilt we feel as we try to balance the time demands of our careers and our families. For example, Mary said, "You feel guilty not spending time with your child, and then feeling guilty spending time with your child and not doing the paper or PowerPoint for class, or whatever.... I found myself in that horrible trap of feeling guilty all the time. It's not realistic." Sentiments of guilt were also expressed as we reflected on our desire to remain in academia. Skye remarked: "I wonder sometimes, okay, do I want to be on the tenure track? Or do I want to be a stay-at-home mom and work part time and adjunct a class? There is guilt there, too—how am I going to tell my advisor that I'm quitting my tenure-track job that I worked so hard to get. So, there's a whole new set of guilt! I feel like there's academic guilt." What Skye coins "academic guilt" is a sentiment we all share. The pressure to not disappoint our advisors and colleagues is an added pressure for academics. Jess noted:

> I think what we're talking about is this idea of disappointing people we care about—whether it's our partner, our children, our advisor, our colleagues. And reading both of your narratives, there were a few things that were pulling at my defensiveness. I take a defensive perspective on motherhood in academia because I feel like I have to. Skye, in your narrative, when your chair was supportive, but you were apologizing for the complication, and I thought that would be me too! I would 110 percent be saying, "I'm sorry, I didn't plan for this. I'm not trying to screw things up for us."

Mary reflected on this sentiment of post-tenure guilt:

> The idea that your pregnancy was a complication and now this big logistic nightmare, that's how I felt with my first pregnancy. With my first pregnancy, I wasn't tenured, but with my second I was. And I have to tell you that when I was not tenured and I was pregnant, it felt like a complication, and it felt like this is a big problem, and that it was embarrassing. But the second time around, I was unapologetic about the whole thing. Like, I'm having a baby, period. It was a statement and not a question. It was different.

Embarrassment

As suggested by the previous excerpt from our conversation, embarrassment evolved as a theme we all related to. Coming out as pregnant while still a graduate student created some embarrassment as noted in Skye's narrative. Moreover, feelings of embarrassment that we would not be able to do our jobs as efficiently as before motherhood manifested in the way we tried not to talk about our pregnancies or motherhood. As Jess explained: "I was nervous to tell [her supervisor at the time] for a couple of reasons ... because I knew I couldn't travel for at least a year. First, because I just didn't want to travel while I was pregnant, and second, I knew my doctor wouldn't have allowed it. Third, I also knew that after my baby was born, I wouldn't want to be away from my baby for at least the first three months." We all gave different yet similar reasons for our nervousness in dealing with our supervisors at those times.

Feelings of embarrassment were also discussed about our pregnant and postpartum bodies. Mary told a story:

Becoming a mother and having children is wonderful and natural, but it's also kind of weird to talk about with your colleagues. One of my male colleagues, a friend, we were talking, and I had mentioned how when I pump, I have to turn the music up really loud because I'm worried about him hearing it [in his office next to mine]. And he's into music and I'm not, so I was making a joke about, sorry I'm blasting the 90s tunes. And he laughed and was shocked, like, why are you embarrassed about it?! And I wanted to say, well, because I'm whipping my breasts out and having a machine suck them four times in a day! It's weird! It's weird and embarrassing but also totally normal. And you're a guy, and I'm sorry. It's just so natural, so expected, so weird. And embarrassing!

The awkwardness of sharing nursing stories with male colleagues was also shared by Jess:

I traveled to a conference when Frances was nine months old, and Frances was still breastfeeding. For that whole weekend, I was so uncomfortable. And I had brought my pump, but it had got to the point where the pump was no good. I was overly uncomfortable, thinking about the discomfort and trying to still be at this conference and talking to people, and I was on the job market. I was traveling with a friend of mine, a guy—and he was just a good enough friend. I had to tell him. I mean, I had to. I didn't have anyone else to tell! I just had to tell him I was so uncomfortable. I couldn't tell strangers at the conference that I'm a breastfeeding mom, and my breasts hurt right now because I haven't nursed! So, I had to tell someone, and I think he was a little uncomfortable. But, ugh, yeah, a moment I'll remember for a while.

We laughed in agreement.

Colliding Worlds

We each identified a challenge in trying to distinguish members of the three separate groups identified above as important to our wellbeing as academics and mothers: our friends, our community, and how our colleagues fit into this picture. Ultimately, we concluded these three separate groups are comprised of the same individuals; in other words, our colleagues are our friends, and this is our community that we heavily rely on. We think these complementary worlds are specific to academia due not only to the intensity of the profession but also to the demands of relocation. Skye reflected:

> You rely on your support.... It was like from day one, [my colleagues] making sure my spring schedule was light, and they weren't giving me too many preps, and I was teaching classes I already taught. And faculty members stepped up to take on my class. All of that, and the baby shower that was thrown. These are strangers, who bought me gifts and were excited for me and couldn't wait to see Alex when he was born and came over to bring food. It was heartwarming and encouraging.

We reflected on the challenges of maintaining relationships in academia with the geographic challenges. Mary elaborated:

> Academia is funny and unique in this sense because we go to school and we have our friends, and we develop really strong friendships in our cohort because no one else knows what it's like. No one gets it unless you're in it, and that's what bonds you to people in the program. And it's great in graduate school, but afterwards it's like, poof! People go all over. My best friend ... if I'm lucky, if I'm not pregnant, I get to see her once a year.... And it's great, and we help each other out and stay in contact, but at the same time, academia is isolating. To have your colleagues and friends all over the world, it's a tight-knit group, but at the same time, that's your only group sometimes.

Finally, we noted how the strength of Jess's academic community, largely comprised of close friends, seemed to minimize many of the challenges Mary and Skye experienced. Although Jess still experienced challenges related to her conflicting academic and motherhood identities, she also reflected how these challenges were experienced with her "village" as a defense weapon. To this point, Jess said, "I think I had a positive experience, and much of it was with thanks to a relatively small group of people in my academic community to make a point to let me know I wasn't alone. I didn't have any negative experiences, but I did have challenges."

Concluding Thoughts

In addition to the themes that emerged from our coffee date, we also spent time discussing the need for greater institutional support. We felt as though the onus was on us, the pregnant faculty members, to learn about and understand maternity leave policies at our institutions and to develop coverage plans. We spent time discussing our friendships as we all journeyed over the often slippery paths of studying while pregnant, or while mothering small children, or what difficulties each of us overcame and continue to battle in academia as professors and mothers. As both professors and mothers, we realize that our friendship forms a supporting community—no matter how small it is and no matter how distant we may be from one another because of the demands of our jobs —and has empowered us to achieve our shared goals. Our friendship has made us aware that the friendship among mothers generates a stable community that fosters stable psycho-emotional and social environments they need to develop and succeed in their mothering and professional careers.

They say it takes a village to raise a child, but maybe in the case of academic mothers, it takes some good colleagues to vent to. Our narratives as three academic mothers who became friends and formed a community based on our experiences as mothers during graduate school have made us realize this: Mothers in academia need to develop a network of academic support to help manage the (sometimes conflicting) identities of mother and scholar. Our time spent reflecting on our lives as mothers and academics has made us aware of the uniqueness of our positions as academic mothers compared to those working mothers in other professions and has helped us become aware that we were not alone because of the friendships we have developed.

Works Cited

Buzzanell, Patrice M., and Suzy D'Enbeau. "Stories of Caregiving: Intersections of Academic Research and Women's Everyday Experiences." *Qualitative Inquiry,* vol. 15, no. 7, 2009, pp. 1199-224.

Fonner, Kathryn L., and Michael E. Roloff. "Testing the Connectivity Paradox: Linking Teleworkers' Communication Media Use to Social Presence, Stress from Interruptions, and Organizational Identification." *Communication Monographs,* vol. 79, no. 2, 2012, pp. 205-31.

Harper, Elizabeth P., et al. "Full-Time Women Faculty Off the Tenure Track: Profile and Practice." *The Review of Higher Education,* vol. 24, no. 3, 2001, pp. 237-257.

Leonardi, Paul M., et al. "The Connectivity Paradox: Using Technology to Both Decrease and Increase Perceptions of Distance in Distributed Work Arrangements." *Journal of Applied Communication Research,* vol. 38, no. 1, 2010, pp. 85-105.

Townsley, Nikki C., and Kirsten J. Broadfoot. "Care, Career, and Academe: Heeding the Calls of a New Professoriate." *Women's Studies in Communication,* vol. 31, no. 2, 2008, pp. 133-42.

Wolfinger, Nicholas H., et al. "Problems in the Pipeline: Gender, Marriage, and Fertility in the Ivory Tower." *The Journal of Higher Education,* vol. 79, no. 4, 2008, pp. 388-405.

Chapter 2

Finding Community as a Mother and a Scholar

Nicole L. Willey

Finding a community had always been relatively easy for me. Even being the new kid in seventh grade didn't cause me too many problems. I was never the most popular, the prettiest, or the richest (in retrospect, thankfully), but I always had a crew. Installed in my new school, my community grew out of Girl Scouts and the long bus rides that took us to new camping spots. In high school, my community became both smaller—one best friend who understood intuitively the need for driving around on country roads screaming out the windows when it all got too much—and more expansive, as marching band, choir, student council, and yearbook introduced me to new people. I rarely think now about that long summer before we all went our separate ways to college; the tears we shed and the nostalgia we felt for the moment we knew was passing.

I was fortunate that in college my best friend and I still had each other, but we added on others—together and separately. Some of those friends were situational communities that formed due to arduous classes and study groups, and some were lifelong. It was easy then to find community. I was the president for SWE—the uncatchy abbreviation for Students for Women's Equality. I worked on the weekly student paper. I travelled through the honours program and found new communities at the University of Guelph and the University of Texas at El Paso. Each time, it was roughly the same: Situational communities cropped up. We ate together, kvetched about dirty dishes together, read the same books together, and got bored in the same classes together. I thought of myself as a gregarious person, often extroverted, and an easy conversationalist. Making friends seemed inevitable. I just returned from a visit with one of the friends I met in El Paso, and now his family is my community, too. Those long-ago communities are fractured by distance, but some of us are still in one another's lives.

Even when I graduated and got my first job as a twelfth grade English teacher at a public high school on the Eastern Shore of Maryland, my community took shape, easily. I now realize the great luck I had in moving into an apartment across from two women and teaching with another, who would become lifelong comrades. We are spread out between Maryland, Ohio, Washington state, and now Kansas, but we check in with one another and try to have reunions every so often. Although it has been twenty-four years since I met these women, the only thing that makes clear how much time has passed when we sporadically see each other is how much bigger our children are. Of course, graduate school provided ready communities as well. I left teaching and went to get my master's degree full time, where I met my husband. Even that felt almost inevitable—if it was hard to find a suitable romantic partner in the real world, perhaps I should go back to school.

I guess I knew even then, or feared, that community would not always be so easy in that "real world." An article in the *New York Times* about making friends as an adult came across my Facebook feed not too long ago. It was published originally in 2012, but with an editor's note saying "We're running it again because the topic is timeless." Timeless indeed. How do adults form communities when, by modern design, the communities we form in school break up due to geography at the end of a fixed period?

As external conditions change, it becomes tougher to meet the three conditions that sociologists since the 1950s have considered crucial to making close friends: proximity; repeated, unplanned interactions; and a setting that encourages people to let their guard down and confide in one another (Williams par. 12). With professional responsibilities, romantic partnerships, and parenting responsibilities, forming friendships as we get older becomes more difficult. My best friend, the one I've known since seventh grade, is now in Colorado, whereas I am in Ohio. The chance of us running into each other by chance, the proximity that allows for shared meals and time to relax together, just doesn't exist without serious time and money expended. We have a commitment to that relationship, and now our families—our husbands and my boys and her girls—form a new community, but one that can only get together once every year or so, if we're fortunate.

Everything seems to come before friends when we make it to adulthood, yet I know I am not alone in craving friendship—comfortable, stimulating, no judgment zones where I can laugh and support and be supported by a group of people who are not my family but my chosen tribe. Unfortunately, in our culture of busyness, maintaining friendships and community is tough; finding and building a community where one doesn't exist can feel impossible. Julie Beck writes:

> Friendships are unique relationships because unlike family relationships, we choose to enter into them. And unlike other voluntary bonds, like marriages and romantic relationships, they lack a formal structure. You wouldn't go months without speaking to or seeing your significant other (hopefully), but you might go that long without contacting a friend. (Beck par. 3)

When so much is a must do, friends can move far down the list of importance. Yet the craving for community, support, and camaraderie is real. In my post student life, having a community has made my "musts" much easier. But as a new faculty member on the tenure track and a new mother, I didn't always have a community. It felt like starting over, and without the situational communities of my past.

I haven't thought about my middle-school experience in a while, but I just re-read Anne Lamott's *Operating Instructions*, and she opens with the fear she has about bringing a child into the world, "knowing full well that he or she is eventually going to have to go through the seventh and eighth grades" (10). Middle school before my move was tough—my then best friend no longer thought I was cool enough for the fifth-grade lunch table; my parents couldn't buy me the Jordache jeans everyone was wearing like it was the law; my general in-between-ness was awkward for me and everyone around me. I had it all: braces, glasses, baby fat, bad hair—I mean really bad hair. Most people I love now completely understand the special hell that the start of middle school, fifth grade, was for me. Lamott says this time was about "feeling completely other ... about hurt and aloneness" (11). Middle-school kids, like my son Jacob, who at this writing is just finishing eighth grade, crave community. They want a place at the table, friends to support them, and people who share their humour and their hurt.

Lamott likens pregnancy to middle school: "the total aloneness in the presence of almost extraterrestrially high levels of hormones" (11). I don't know if this feeling is universal, but for Lamott and me, becoming a mother felt like middle school all over again. My hormones and moods were outside of my comfortable ranges; I had friends who cared about me and my son, but for a variety of reasons—geography, a different place in life—I didn't have friends who would drop in unannounced to lend an ear or take my baby for a while. Unlike Lamott, I was fortunate to have my partner, the father of my now eighth and fifth graders. He was there to support me and make me laugh. My family was also supportive, thrilled, and excited about my expected child. Although I appreciated my sisters' phone calls and my mom's e-mails, and our sporadic visits, they were too far-flung to provide the physical presence I craved so much. Perhaps I was greedy, but I wanted more—more adult conversation, less time fully on my own with my gorgeous baby. Even though I was thirty-one when I had Jacob, most of my close friends (at that point, all many hours driving distance from me) had not yet started having babies themselves, so in addition to physical distance, we had experiential differences to bridge. Most mothers know how hard it is to have a conversation on the phone when young children are present, and I felt needy and self-conscious calling my friends who weren't yet mothers. I needed their presence, but I also couldn't attend to it when I had it.

I am on the other side of becoming a mother by fourteen years now. When I became pregnant, I was in my second year of a tenure-track appointment at the university where I am still employed. We had moved sixteen hours from our graduate program in Alabama, leaving our friends behind. We learned quickly that the blue-collar town we moved to considers people who have only been there for decades to be newcomers. Virtually everyone I met outside of the university had what seemed like three generations deep of family connections; everyone I met inside the university was already an established scholar, and if they were mothers, they were no longer new to that job. I was reading everything about motherhood I could get my hands on, but very little of the approved works spoke to me. Without a nearby community of mothers, I was floundering.

When a book that showed me what should happen each week of my pregnancy scared me, I threw it across the room. I rolled my eyes at *What to Expect When You're Expecting* when I read the diet I should follow for the baby's optimum health. I didn't have pregnant or new moms around me in real life, and I didn't have them around me virtually either. The books and magazines I found didn't help, and I hadn't yet found blogs or social media to help round out the experience. Luckily, my husband got me a subscription to *Brain, Child*, which restored some of my faith in finding thoughtful, complicated, and likeminded mothers. And then I found *Operating Instructions*. My new world broke open. Lamott was so wonderfully irreverent, hilarious, and awestruck. She put words to my fears and my hopes. She made me feel something like a community.

I just read the book again because not everyone in my book club had. I don't remember whose idea it was, but that never matters. There are five of us. We are all moms of children at different stages. Our kids range from five to twenty-five. We are all educators, but at different places, levels, and disciplines. We represent English, philosophy, math, science, and business; we teach elementary school, high school, and college to students in vocational, gifted, traditional, and nontraditional programs in-person and online. We have a variety of familial configurations and different social circles. We came together due to an alchemy of anti-Trump organizing and social media, and we all feel quite lucky to have found each other. If you had told me fourteen years ago that it would take that long to find my local community of moms, I would have cried, or perhaps it would have given me hope. We get together monthly, sometimes with families but mostly without. The connection that was forged about two years ago has become a frequent messenger group presence as well as a welcome respite from our normal professional lives. Recently, when my husband and I had yet another scheduling snafu, my group came to the rescue, offering to help with rides for my kids. That may seem small, but these women have lifted a huge weight from me, the weight of feeling like I'm in this life alone. To me, these women and our new connections are a miracle.

One of the members just this morning mentioned in our group message that the most powerful part of Lamott for her was the community she built around her mothering. I don't remember focusing on that part so acutely with my first read, but with this read, Lamott's people feel like, and she labels them as, a miracle. I understand this miracle more fully now than I did in those early days when I still held onto the hope that finding my community was just around the corner. And in some ways, it was. When I was a new mom, I found other new moms through library programs and friends of friends. We'd schedule playdates for our babies that were really for us to not feel so alone. But those early connections forged around our children didn't last, for reasons like moving or political differences or simply the ways our kids didn't end up choosing each other when they could make their own friendship choices.

What sustained me for the twelve or so years before I found my people? Of course, my husband, and my growing family. Our extended families. Some good friends who despite not being in the same situation with parenting loved our kids and filled in with babysitting and card games. A family who although they moved away were and still are in the same experiential place; we provide a place for them to land twice a year. Eventually, my whole family found a group of three other families who have a supper club, complete with food themes, about once a month. Our kids (mostly) get along while the adults play games and laugh. Those connections are growing as time goes on, and we are thankful for them as well. The kinship there comes from shared experience, professional connections, time, and the fact that we have all committed to setting up the next meeting before we leave the current one. Considering all the variables of partners and kids and the nuanced dynamics that are produced, we consider this group a miracle as well.

But before book club and supper club, and in between friends' visits and sporadic game nights with friends who became aunts and uncles to our kids, there was a lot of alone time. A lot of overusing *Max and Ruby* and *Scholastic* video DVDs. A lot of concern that not only would I (and we as a family) not find a stable local community but that the rigours of early motherhood would derail my professional life. I had my first baby in my second year on the tenure track. During the third year—the crucial one that demanded verified scholarly fruits for my labours—I got rejection after rejection, and I panicked. I'd rock Jacob late into the night, wondering if I would ever actually get published. Was I wasting my baby's early moments only to fail at securing tenure? Was I, in fact, just an impostor in a world I had no business entering?

Brene Brown notes that "Depression and anxiety are two of the body's first reactions to stockpiles of hurt" (64). I wasn't depressed exactly, but the anxiety was doing a number on me. I'd nurse in a daze, partly due to sleep deprivation from my baby who woke anywhere from three to five times a night. But part of my daze—my inability to appreciate the (now long lost) moments with my son, where he'd hold my finger with his whole hand and look in my eyes—had to do with anxiety. Even if he had been sleeping through the night, I wouldn't have been. As any academic knows, and many will admit, rejection letters are a particularly harsh form of hazing. I occasionally got a kind editor, but I got what felt like more than my share of mean peer reviewers, and their comments left me numb.

Who did I think I was? How could I ever join a community of academics when I didn't even know how to string sentences together, let alone think abstractly? Brown points out that one way out of internalized hurt is "integrating": "There's growing empirical evidence that not owning and integrating our stories affects not just our emotional health but also our physical well-being" (67). What I was doing—worrying and rehashing old work (both in the sense that it was my previous work, and it was academically traditional)—was decidedly not working. It was time to find a new path, and, for me, that ultimately meant integrating my personal stories and interests with my academic ones. In The Motherhood Initiative for Research and Community Involvement (MIRCI)—now IAMAS (International Association of Maternal Action and Scholarship) and formerly Association for Research On Mothering (ARM)—and Demeter Press, I have found a supportive and positive academic mothering community, a community that somehow had eluded me while I was paralyzed under the spell of publishing anxiety due to bad feedback on my previous work. MIRCI, and now IAMAS, provide an academic mothers' community and a forum for my voice; more than that, the women of those organizations helped me find my voice. For this mother, my path to professional success, the success that enabled me to keep my job and ultimately find my local communities, was about integrating my personal life with my academic life; in writing my stories into my scholarship, I became a better version of myself—personally and professionally. And for me to write this more integrated person into existence, I needed community. My foremothers and sisters, led by Andrea O'Reilly and now Katie Garner, have given me an academic home.

I became the first female full professor on my campus in 2017. My full professorship bid was supported unanimously by my regional campus as well as my department, which happens to be the English Department at Kent State University. I would not have been able to reach this institutional summit in my career if it were not for MIRCI and Demeter. This is not an overstatement. I may not have even earned tenure, or landed my job in the first place, without this body. Furthermore, the work I have done, work which feeds me, has been in the service of shedding light on the importance of mother's voices, marginalized mother's voices, and the voices of academics coming out as mothers, as a force for change. My career as a scholar and eventually as an academic mother has been shaped in every way by the work done by this community of academic mothers that I feel so fortunate to have joined. And this community let me in before I was an academic or a mother.

As a young scholar working on my master's thesis, I discovered Andrea O'Reilly, but at this point through her work only. She and Marianne Hirsch gave voice to the struggle I was having—to focus not on the daughter's vision of the mother but the mother herself through the motherline. I turned part of that thesis into an article early in my PhD program, and although I felt scared and scarcely ready to share my work with anyone, I sent an abstract to the ARM conference that was taking place in 2000. I was accepted, my department gave me 500 dollars, and I was on my way to having my work heard. I remember feeling both excited and overwhelmed, recognizing that there was so much work that needed to be done in this field, and I was nervous about the fact that I knew I wanted to be a part of it. I also knew my department wasn't very keen on interdisciplinary work, but I still sent a full article: "Ibuza vs. Lagos: The Feminist and Traditional Buchi Emecheta" to the *Journal for the Association for Research on Mothering* (*JARM*). This was my first publication. Between the conference and the publication, I felt finally validated as a scholar.

I accepted my current position at Kent State University Tuscarawas in 2003, after wondering whether I would get a position in the (always) glutted English job market. It was tenure-track with a 4/4 load and "better" than what many of my cohort were managing. Like many academic women, I started my first job around the same time I was seriously (and finally) considering becoming a mother. As a new mother with Jacob, I couldn't find any literature that spoke to me about mothering in academia; it was at a Northeast Modern Language Association (NeMLA) conference in 2007 that I met Justine Dymond. Her daughter was two, my baby was not yet one, and my breasts were aching through that whole conference—Jacob didn't come with me, and even pumping didn't relieve the strain of being away from him. Our book, published by Demeter in 2013 called *Motherhood Memoirs; Mothers Creating/Writing Lives*, was conceived in the hallway at that conference.

I had flouted the unwritten rules for women on the tenure track at Kent State by having not one but two children in my probationary period. Academic tolling to extend the probationary period for new faculty to publish work and get tenure didn't exist for me during my first pregnancy. Without a community of other academic mothers nearby, I had no models. I fantasized about converting to nontenure track, where I wouldn't have to complete research. At this point, I was mostly still trying to get my nineteenth-century Americanist work published, and I was having lousy luck. The work felt dead to me too, so it wasn't ever a complete surprise when it got rejected. I was exhausted and milk engorged and barely surviving in my teaching, let alone having time to write and think. My job was in danger. I remember thinking that this would all be worth it if I get tenure, but if I spend my children's baby years stressing out and still don't keep the job, I wouldn't know how to handle the anger and regret. It was in this state of mind that I saw a call for papers from *JARM* that coincided with a new idea. I sent in my essay, "Mothering in Slavery: A Revision of African Feminist Principles," and it was accepted. Before this, my only publication since being hired had been an article about teaching—my real life at the regional campus—but the pedagogical scholarship was frowned upon by many of my colleagues. This one article in *JARM* gave me hope and courage. I reworked my dissertation in the way it needed, and it became a book. Tenure was secure.

NeMLA again played a role in my motherhood studies career when I presented the paper "Body *and* Mind: Pregnancy and Motherhood, Twice, Before Tenure" at the Buffalo conference in 2008. This paper was the first time I publicly admitted to some of the tenure-track terror I experienced. Justine had created that panel, and we were meeting women that would ultimately contribute to our book. I fondly remember a group of us finding dinner one night in Buffalo, and Andrea O'Reilly convincing us all to share our birth stories at the table. Isaac, my second son, was one month old and in the hotel room with his brother and father, and I was relieved to get back and nurse him, but I knew that I had found my scholar sisters that night.

My husband and I got tenure and our first promotions. We raised our babies. We spent a lot of time being tired, but the stress over job security had passed, and I, for the first time, found myself devoted to research that was for me. I wanted to work on it because I wanted to help usher into the world the kind of writing about mothering that I wanted to read. Eventually securing two publications post-tenure and the publication of my collection with Justine, I started to realize I might build a record for promotion to full professor. After all, with the book, I now had a keynote speaker credit, and two other invited talks related to our book.

Regional campus faculty at Kent State University hold tenure in the regional system, but our promotions are held in the department. Therefore, although our teaching loads are roughly twice that of Kent campus faculty, and we have little to no access to graduate students, our promotion criteria are the same as if our campus missions were the same. There is no time pressure for the full professor bid, but I began to be hungry for the recognition (and pay—no small thing) that my scholarship was incrementally making me eligible for. I was in a position where I could choose my projects carefully and according to my passions. I also knew that my fields post-tenure—memoir, maternal narrative, motherhood studies—along with my particular scholarly voice, one that is personal and subjective and uses auto theory as opposed to more traditional scholarship, were not widely understood in my department at large. I kept writing anyway. Eventually, I had enough scholarship and citations to prove that sought after national/international reputation, and I had it largely due to work I had done with and through *JARM* and Demeter Press as well as through Routledge collections through networks I found at MIRCI conferences. My promotion dossier proved that motherhood studies is interdisciplinary and cutting edge and has political power and urgency.

The history of my involvement with this academic/mothering community shows its role in my professional success, but I still wish to emphasize just how important this community has been to my mental and emotional health and development as a scholar and a mother. Justine and I created a community of people I learned from, shared with, and respect within our memoir collection. We did most of our work on that book when our children were still young. I was still lactating for large portions of the writing, and I felt a lifeline had been extended to me through the writing of these women, many of whom were also writing about mothering young children. As I have aged and my mothering has become more about the middle—the middle of my children's childhoods, the middle of my life—I have found solace in working on the *Mothering in Midlife* collection from Demeter. And as my ideas about mothering boys have taken turns toward combating toxic masculine culture, I have learned from and expanded my ideas about mothering and scholarship through contributing to the *Mothers and Sons*, *Pops in Pop Culture* collections, and the recently published *Feminist Fathering* collection I coedited. At each step, editors and writers have helped me hone my voice and expand my knowledge. While I've probably only met about one-quarter of this community in person, the community stretches from Canada to Australia to Spain to Wales, as well as across the United States, and gives me sustenance and hope. This community is also a miracle.

And now it is my turn to take the lead in community building—on my campus and in my discipline. I have been asked to be an external reviewer for tenure and promotion cases. I have reviewed books and written blurbs. I am a blind peer reviewer for several journals, and I always strive to be helpful as opposed to mean. As a steering committee member for the newly formed IAMAS, I continue to work with academic sisters while striving to provide a place for maternal voices and action. On my campus, I am the mentor program coordinator, and as I grow into this role, I think a lot about fostering community within smaller cohorts and as a whole. I do my best to bring people together so as to help them not feel so alone in academia. Some of these communities include mothers, and I almost always find that our conspiratorial friendships grow deeper than many others—we get it. We don't all mother the same way or in the same circumstances, but we empathize with the struggles and the joys.

I feel lucky to have gotten to this place. Having an eighth grader and a fifth grader, I have more physical freedom. They can stay home by themselves, bathe themselves, and feed themselves; their independence feels like a reward for those early days. Having secured tenure and my final promotion gives me time too, time to pick the projects I most care about, time to serve in ways that are meaningful on my campus and in the discipline. I have time now for socializing with my various communities, and I have the institutional leverage to help create communities. This will continue to be my work, to help others, and, selfishly, to help myself as well.

Works Cited

Beck, Julie. "How Friendships Change Over Time in Adulthood." *The Atlantic*, 22 Oct. 2015, www.theatlantic.com/health/archive/2015/10/how-friendships-change-over-time-in-adulthood/411466/. Accessed 12 Feb. 2022.

Brown, Brene. *Rising Strong: How the Ability to Resent Transforms the Way we Live, Love, Parent, and Lead*. Random House, 2017.

Byrd, Marilyn Y. "Social Identity Diversity and Leadership in the Workforce." *Diversity in the Workforce: Current Issues and Encouraging Trends*, edited by Marilyn Y. Byrd and Chanda L. Scott, Routledge, 2018, chapter 17, Kindle version.

Lamott, Anne. *Operating Instructions: A Journal of My Son's First Year*. Anchor Books, 1993.

Ward, Adrian. "Meeting to Learn and Learning to Meet." *Intuition Is Not Enough: Matching Learning With Practice in Therapeutic Child Care*, edited by Adrian Ward and Linnet McMahon, Routledge, 1998, pp. 88-120.

Williams, Alex. "The Challenge of Making Friends as an Adult." *New York Times*, 15 July 2012, www.nytimes.com/2012/07/15/fashion/the-challenge-of-making-friends-as-an-adult.html. Accessed 12 Feb. 2022.

Chapter 3

Mothers, Mentors, and Communities in Alice Walker's *The Color Purple* and Sapphire's *Push*

Zsuzsanna Lénárt-Muszka

Sapphire's novel *Push* (1996) has been credited as referencing a multitude of literary predecessors both in its evocation of incest, invisibility, or the use of the oral tradition (Fulton 164-65; Michlin 171; Dagbovie-Mullins 446; McNeil 24). Although Ralph Ellison's classic novel, *Invisible Man* (1952), or some of Toni Morrison's novels can certainly be established as predecessors, *Push* undoubtedly draws the most influence from Alice Walker's *The Color Purple* (1982). These novels have been compared for their plot structures, narrative styles, and the social significance of education and literacy. However, an aspect that has largely gone unexamined so far is their parallels regarding the importance of the maternal in mentorship, friendship, and community. The emotional and often material support offered by other women in both *The Color Purple* and *Push* aid the protagonists—Celie and Precious, respectively—in developing and obtaining self-worth and obtaining degrees of independence. More specifically, I argue, it helps them to reclaim ownership of their bodies after traumatic experiences and, thus, to come to terms with their motherhood. Mentorship and friendship become politicized in both texts to illustrate the long-lasting economic and sexual exploitation of African American women's bodies, reminiscent of slavery. After briefly introducing and contextualizing the novels with a focus on the traumas and the lived experience of motherhood for both protagonists, I argue that mentors and communities, organized in various ways, give Celie and Precious validation and allow them to carve out spaces for themselves and to circumvent the system of interlocking oppressions.

Even though they were written about protagonists far removed in time and space, the statements *The Color Purple* and *Push* make with regards to Black motherhood are strikingly similar. The former novel is set in rural Georgia, US, in deep poverty, decades after the abolition of slavery, in the first third of the twentieth century. African American people were legally free citizens; nevertheless, they were severely disenfranchised economically and were subject to blatant racism. This was evident in, among others, racial segregation and lynching, which happened with shocking regularity in the Southern US. Not only were Black women victims of this race- and class-based oppression, but they were also marginalized on account of their gender. *The Color Purple* thematizes all of these issues through the plight of its narrator-protagonist, Celie, an African American woman who is a teenager at the beginning of the plot. She is regularly raped by her father, Alphonso, who impregnates her twice, but the babies are taken away from her. Celie is forced into a marriage with an older man, named Mr., who also exploits her. However, she gradually gains enough strength to abandon her abuser, confront her stepfather, and learn to support herself financially. Finally, she reunites with her children and her sister, Nettie.

Precious, the narrator-protagonist of *Push*, has a similar trajectory. She is an African American teenager living in Harlem at the end of the twentieth century. Her father rapes her repeatedly; as a result, she becomes pregnant at the ages of twelve and sixteen and has two traumatic birth experiences. She suffers from physical abuse and severe emotional neglect. She lives in poverty and is illiterate until she gets into the fictional program called Each One Teach One, whose goal is to assist youth deemed problematic by the education system. The novel offers an optimistic and a cathartic ending: after forging a new identity by confronting her mother, among others, Precious reconnects with her children.

By introducing disenfranchised, exploited protagonists who get pregnant against their will, both novels interrogate how oppression has been inscribed within the constructs and narratives of Black womanhood and motherhood since slavery. They offer a reconfiguration of the meanings of female communities within the African American experience. During slavery, long-lasting, tightly knit communities scarcely existed. A large number of slaves were bought and sold at such a fast rate that it made the forging of emotional bonds difficult. Hierarchy existed insofar as slaves had different responsibilities on plantations, for example, the status of field hands differed from that of house slaves (Schneider 111). Older plantation slaves, operators of the underground railroad, or those who assisted runaways and newly free people in the North could be considered mentors, but no official, organized way of mentorship existed. Both *The Color Purple* and *Push* signify this feature of social interaction by introducing protagonists who are treated very much like slaves, yet whose lives are improved greatly by their mentors and communities.

Both texts are trauma narratives; thus, the rape and abuse of Celie and Precious have direct implications on how they perceive their bodies and motherhood. They undergo a similar process of conceptualizing and experiencing their pregnancies. Both get pregnant when they are teens, under traumatic circumstances, and due to the major lack of educational and healthcare resources, they do not understand the biological processes that happen to them. Only gradually do Celie and Precious come to understand that they are not responsible for getting pregnant. *The Color Purple* and *Push* illustrate how fundamental an effect the interlocking oppressions of race, class, and gender can have on being a mother. Their economic and sexual exploitation illustrates what Steven Martinot describes as the denigration of Black maternal bodies to political instruments that serve the interest of white supremacy through cementing inequality. Martinot argues that slavery narrativized (and redefined) African (that is, African American) motherhood as economic production to be able to represent English and white American motherhood as "cultural production" (86). In Martinot's reading, denigrating the Black maternal body was instrumental to elevating the white maternal body and positing it as dignified; in a more general sense, it was an essential factor in the "construction of a white racialized identity" (86). Toni Morrison puts forward a similar argument: The "ego-reinforcing presence of [the] African population" contributed to the positive "self-definition" of white America (45).

Thus, these processes of the systematic dehumanization of Black mothers have served white patriarchal political ends: they inscribed the white, American body as normal at the expense of the racialized, gendered other.

In the deep South stricken by Jim Crow laws and patriarchy, the knowledge Celie is given regarding motherhood forms the basis of how she will later think about her status as a mother. Her earliest information about what it means to be a mother comes from the exchanges between Alphonso and his wife: "Last spring after little Lucious come I heard them fussing. He was pulling on her arm. She say It too soon, Fonso, I ain't well. Finally he leave her alone. A week go by, he pulling on her arm again. She say Naw, I ain't gonna. Can't you see I'm already half dead, an all of these children?" (Walker 4-5). After learning about the toll motherhood takes on the body, Celie warns her sister about it. When she says, "and look what happen to Ma" (7), she refers not only to her death but also to the above conversation as well. When her mother starts suspecting that her husband has been raping Celie, "she ast me bout the first one Whose it is? I say God's. I don't know no other man or what else to say" (5). Celie's answer evades confronting her ill mother with the truth, but in part, it stems from an earnest ignorance of biology. She rests assured that she cannot get pregnant when "a girl at church say you git big if you bleed every month" because her menstruation has stopped (7). The wisdom shared among women that might otherwise prove to be a useful tool is only available in bits and gets misinterpreted not only because Celie's oppressive domestic environment isolates her from her peers but also because those peers live in similar subjugation due to a systemic lack of resources. This lack stands in the way of her understanding of what is happening to her. The only bit of information Celie seems to know for sure is that pregnancy and its horrors are inevitable: "I say Marry him, Nettie, an try to have one good year out your life. After that, I know she be big," (7) and "I know right then the next thing I hear, she be big" (31). Even years after her rape, she confesses: "I tried to work on some new pants I'm trying to make for pregnant women, but just the thought of anybody gitting pregnant make me want to cry" (306). This visceral reaction testifies to the long-lasting impact of her trauma.

In *The Color Purple*, men look at women as mere objects, parts of the environment; consequently, this gaze is internalized. Mr. not only physically abuses Celie but also erases her subjectivity by denying her humanness when he looks at her "like he looking at the earth" (23). When he is beating her, Celie's survival tactic consists of the internalization of this dehumanization: "I make myself wood. I say to myself, Celie, you a tree" (24). Ironically, though, she admits that this dislocation cannot guarantee her escape: "That's how come I know trees fear man" (24). As a consequence of the alienation from her body, she starts perceiving other people as being objects as well: "Patting Harpo back not even like patting a dog. It more like patting another piece of wood. Not a living tree, but a table, a chifferobe" (30). Due to the instrumentalization of the female body, women's complex subjectivity becomes invisible. The sizable belly of the pregnant woman becomes her only visible feature; thus, it becomes a metonymy as it repeatedly stands in for her. Discussion regarding motherhood is buried in a set of metonymies, such as the matryoshka doll, which symbolizes the inability to conceptualize motherhood in complex terms. Far from being an innocent figure of speech, the metonymy of the big belly contributes to the effacement of the subjectivities of these already battered women through the association of a part of the pregnant female anatomy with the expectant mother herself.

In this context of dehumanization and fear of motherhood, Celie's maternal identification is a complex process. Despite her lack of education and her fear of becoming "big," she has some reaffirming, positive experiences with early motherhood. When her first baby is born, she is swept away by the experience despite all the hardships: "When I start to hurt and then my stomach start moving and then that little baby come out my pussy chewing on it fist you could have knock me over with a feather" (5-6). Later, she remembers and acknowledges that she enjoyed the intimacy of breastfeeding: "I haul up my dress and look at my titties. Think bout my babies sucking them. Remember the little shiver I felt then too. Sometimes a big shiver. Best part about having the babies was feeding 'em" (81). Thus, even though she lacks knowledge of anatomy and having babies is posited as a physically and emotionally[1] taxing chore, the instinctual enjoyment is still present. The social order she is subjugated in robs her of it. Her situation, then—being kept in the dark and in fear, coupled with her children being taken from her—resembles slavery. Just as slaves became chattels and were denied their personal and communal history, Celie is shut off from the communal or familial knowledge and human relationships that could help her make sense of the effects of motherhood. A further parallel with slavery is that although the novel interrogates "being big" and the postpartum period, depictions of caring for children are few and far between, as slave women were often traumatically separated from their infants. In the diegetic universe, it is only the mothering of African women, and only before colonization, that is not intermittent or disturbed by patriarchy, economic constraints, or violence. Even though various patterns of mothering exist in the novel, most of them are deeply traumatizing.

A major factor in Celie's process of subject formation is her multifaceted attachment to Shug, her husband's former lover. Shug's influence is wide-reaching, and her lessons are varied. Celie gets encouragement and gentleness from their intimate lesbian relationship, and Shug also teaches her business skills by encouraging her to make and sell pants for women. Moreover, her role as a mother figure is significant. The extent to which Celie needs a strong and supportive maternal presence in her life after years of being tortured by men is evident in her relief when they make up after a fight, and Celie "sleeps like a baby" (43). Her babylike status is reaffirmed when she remarks that the intimacy they share reminds her of her mother: "Me and Shug sound asleep. Her back to me, my arms round her waist. What it like? Little like sleeping with mama" (121-22). But this feeling is reciprocated, as Shug is reminded of maternal figures when she is leaning against Celie's knees (53). Another side of their intense relationship is encapsulated by Linda Abbandonato's phrase "sisters in spirit" (1111). Shug becomes the "undoer of inessential and divisive hierarchies" (Hite 126) so that the enmeshment of the familial and the erotic gestures towards incestuous desires. But as Abbandonato points out, this enmeshment results at the same time in the dissolution of taboos (1111).

The trope of motherhood is apparent in another process that helps Celie and, in fact, the other traumatized mothers as well—finding strength in establishing a community in which women and mothers feel at ease in the presence of one another. To adopt a term used by philosophers Gilles Deleuze and Félix Guattari, this is a rhizomatically organized community (6-10). The concept of the rhizome, borrowed from botany, refers to a specific organizational pattern of ideas, knowledge, theory, research, and culture in general. Instead of developing linearly and vertically, the rhizome, a kind of stem, grows in multiple directions. Therefore, it can be considered a metaphor for structures that are not hierarchical. Instead of having a specific origin and centre, these structures have several nodes as well as multiple entry and exit points with multiple kinds, levels, and intensities of interpersonal relationships. When, for example, Sofia is incarcerated, her husband's lover attempts to set her free and even looks after her children; in this scenario, there are at least seven people who are in a complicated relationship with one another, all of them being friends or family members of Celie. Celie also has different kinds of attachments to Shug, since she is her husband's lover while also being married. Instead of making up a hierarchical community, these people form a unique web, reminiscent of the community model theorized by Hortense Spillers (75-76). This new model makes visible the inherent dysfunctionality of hierarchical, patriarchal family structures, the undoing of which suggests the necessity of an ethics of care that privileges communal child-rearing. Patricia Hill Collins asserts that "in confronting racial oppression, maintaining community-based childcare and respecting othermothers who assume child-care responsibilities can serve a critical function in African-American communities"[2] (*Black Feminist Thought* 180). These structures were necessitated by the intended destruction of Black families and communities during slavery.[3]

The women involved in this community share different kinds of work, which provide Celie with solace. It also offers her a reconceptualization of "work," which was used to degrade women and their domestic responsibilities by Harpo (23). The tasks they perform in synchronicity are described idyllically: "Me and Sofia piecing another quilt together. I got bout five squares pieced, spread out on the table by my knee. My basket full of scraps on the floor" (56). This setting gives Celie so much comfort that she can feel competent in the presence of her former abuser too: "I see myself sitting there quilting tween Shug Avery and Mr. Us three set together against Tobias and his fly speck box of chocolate. For the first time in my life, I feel just right" (58). This collaboration takes the form of sharing the responsibilities of taking care of children (255), showing Walker's vision of womanist mothering relying upon the system of shared childcare Black women have often engaged in (Collins, "Black Women and Motherhood" 152-53). Far from the white middle-class ideal of the mother-child dyad and the nuclear family, womanism echoes the system of othermothering in "embracing extended familial and communal bonds, drawing from traditional African gender roles, kinship ties and definitions of community to build a 'village' that shares in child-rearing responsibilities" (Abdullah 58). This culminates in Celie taking ownership of her children that Nettie has been raising: "I am so happy. I got love, I got work, I got money, friends and time. And you alive and be home soon. With *our* children" (my emphasis, Walker 250). By having another woman as a mentor as well as by being part of a community, Celie heals from the trauma caused by sexual abuse and being separated from her children. Reclaiming her body leads her to reappropriate her motherhood, which is a crucial step in her becoming her own agent.

A similar process of traumatization and reappropriation takes place in the case of another Black teen in *Push*. *The Color Purple* is a major point of reference within the diegetic universe of the novel, and its structure and plot points are also in conversation. *Push* is set after the Civil Rights Movements, in an era in which institutional networks are supposed to safeguard the disenfranchised and protect the most marginalized individuals—all accomplishments which were unthinkable in the Southern US decades earlier. Instead of aiding Precious, institutions such as the education system and child protective services marginalize and fail her while further traumatizing her.

Precious's trauma and the subsequent alienation from her body mirror those of Celie. Not only is she isolated and sexually, verbally, and physically abused by her parents, but she is also animalized by the limited number of people with whom she is in contact. Her father calls Precious a heifer while raping her and slaps her thigh "like cowboys do horses on TV" (Sapphire 27); her classmates bully her by making "fart sounds" and "hog grunt sounds" (41). Her academic performance as a child and as a teenager suffers because of her abuse: She cannot concentrate. She is often in a pathological dissociative state and cannot even establish contact with her teachers or her peers. As she is too traumatized to move, she is left sitting in her urine (41). She has an extremely limited way of expressing herself. One of the first instances of her attempting to emote in any way occurs after her father rapes her, and she is deeply ashamed of the positive physical sensations she experiences. She feels compelled to smear her face with fecal matter in an attempt to reconnect with her body: "Afterward I go bafroom. I smear shit on my face. Feel good. Don't know why but it do" (121).

Precious thinks of being a mother with the same disgust as Celie does. The maternal body is pathologized in *Push* in the sense that it is undesirable to the point of being revolting. Precious describes the ideal body as one that is a virgin yet looks like the hypersexualized body of superstar Whitney Houston (124), which signals her escape fantasies (Dagbovie-Mullins 441). Then, she elaborates on physical characteristics connected to being a mother that she finds disturbing: "I would be a tight pussy girl no stretch marks and torn pussy from babies's head bust me open" (124). The daydreams in which she fantasizes about being similar to celebrities whose bodies are very far from being maternal serve a double function. The daydreams are often triggered by sexual activity (Dagbovie-Mullins 441)—that is, they help Precious to dissociate while being raped. I would also would argue that these fantasies reflect Precious's conviction that becoming a mother is inevitable, and it is only in her fantasies that she can have control over her body, which echoes the similar processes in *The Color Purple*. In the next few lines, she offers a summary of her point of view on what constitutes acceptable: "One time boy come to Advancement House to see girlfriend, he think I'm somebody's mother. That bother me" (124). Her discomfort may in part be because she is mistaken for someone much older than she is; for her, also, being a mother and being attractive are mutually exclusive.

Hatred for herself as a mother is also interwoven with the hatred that she feels towards her mother. At first, Precious associates motherhood with her mother even after she gives birth: "I like light-skin people, they nice. I likes slim people too. Mama fat black, if I weigh two hundred she weigh three" (33). However, Precious cannot help but identify with her to the point that she seems to think her mother is some kind of a doppelganger to her, the embodiment of the characteristics that she cannot accept about herself: "Sometimes I pass by store window and somebody fat dark skin, old looking, someone look like my muver look back at me. But I know it can't be my muver 'cause my muver is at home" (35). This unwitting, unwanted identification with a dreaded mother is suggestive of Precious's matrophobia—a concept coined by Lynn Sukenick and Adrienne Rich—regarding the fear of becoming one's mother (Rich 235). In the words of Rich:

"Where a mother is hated to the point of matrophobia there may also be a deep underlying pull toward her, a dread that if one relaxes one's guard one will identify with her completely" (235). Thus, when Precious is mistaken for a woman her mother's age and later needs cognitive effort to remind herself that she is not the same person as her mother after catching a glimpse of her reflection in the store window, she realizes she cannot relax her guard.

What links Celie's and Precious's experience in the early days of mothering is that they would benefit from being part of a community of mothers who could provide them with positive models not only regarding child-rearing but in terms of what the maternal body looks like. In lieu of positive reinforcement, however, Precious is revolted by her own changing body. She is critical of her mother's obesity yet feels that her looks have been influenced by the physical manifestation of motherhood—going through pregnancy and breastfeeding. The way she scrutinizes her maternal body—"Who I see? I stand in tub sometime, look my body, it stretch marks, ripples" (36)—is reminiscent of how Celie observes her breasts (Walker 81). However, whereas Celie links what she sees to empowering maternal experiences, Precious remains anxious about her stretch marks caused by pregnancy. This unease underlines that she is still alienated from her corporeal experiences due to trauma.

Precious's dissociation from her pregnant body and the fetus also underscores her tendency to perceive her body as abnormal. Lacking the resources—be they educational, familial, or communal—that could help her understand her pregnant body better, Precious is an expectant mother only in a biological sense. Probably because of the traumatic nature of her first birth, she is not looking forward to it and she does not have a connection to the fetus. She also constitutes it as something menacing because it has a life of its own. Precious's belated maternal attachment might undoubtedly be due to the circumstances of conception as the detachment from her pregnant body mirrors the alienation she feels when she is being raped: "This baby feel like a watermelon between my bones getting bigger and my ankles feelin' tight cause they swoled" (64-65), and it is "something stuck in me, growing in me, making me bigger" (70). The malevolent image of the ever-expanding watermelon that is about to burst suggests that Precious conceptualizes her pregnant body as a host of something threatening as well as something alien to her, having been seized by an alien teleology (Lundquist 142). As a result, she oscillates between indifference and a sense of horror.

Another character who is dehumanized in the novel is Precious's first child, Mongo, who also becomes a part of Precious's assuming a new sense of self. Mongo was born with Down syndrome and is failed by the healthcare system; instead of getting appropriate care, she is allowed to live with Precious's grandmother, who exploits her for welfare benefits (36; 62). The institution of othermothering, often prevalent in African American communities (Collins, *Black Feminist Thought* 129), is thus corrupted and fails to provide Precious with much-needed communal support. Precious's mother also says that it is not worth putting any effort into parenting or caring for the child since she is disabled. As Precious explains: "I hardly have not seen my daughter since she was a little baby. I never stick my bresses in her mouth. My muver say what for? It's outta style. She say I never do you. What that child of yours need tittie for? She retarded. Mongoloid. Down Sinder" (36). Despite the messages she gets from her mother about breastfeeding, she can enjoy bonding with Abdul, her second child: "I like baby I born. It gets to suckes from my bress. First I don't like that. It hurt feel sore, then I like it" (77). Eventually, she starts to consider the possibility of getting Mongo back from her grandmother.

Even though she is slow to embrace her maternal self, how Precious relates to pregnancy evolves significantly while she also starts occupying her body and listening to its signals. The comfort Precious derives from having physical contact with Abdul can finally mirror what Celie feels. The process of reclaiming motherhood and selfhood through the body reaches full circle when Precious connects with her son in a scene at the end of the narrative. The last image of the novel is one of Precious sitting with her son on her lap and reading him a story, which happens after she understands the potency of language and storytelling through, among others, reading about Celie. She uses language to transmit knowledge, which is a new and powerful ability for her. However, reading to a child on one's lap is as much a bodily practice as it is an emotional or cognitive one; the connection that is established through touch can be just as potent as sharing ideas. Celie also heals through the body; for her, it is the physical and emotional gentleness and sensual care she gets from another woman that helps her.

The relationship Precious has with Ms. Rain, the maternal figure who becomes her mentor, resembles the connection Celie has with Shug, albeit without homoerotic undertones. According to Monica Michlin, "There is no lesbian love story in *Push*, in part due to the choice of the narrator (Sapphire certainly did not want Ms. Rain to be perceived as seducing Precious), but also, perhaps, because the anxiety of influence associated with [*The Color Purple*] was too intense, dissuading Sapphire from trying to create a love story that would compete with Celie's and Shug's" (183). Apart from teaching Precious to write, introducing her to literature (most notably, to *The Color Purple*), and assisting her with finding accommodation, it is Rain's insistence that Precious love herself that has the most effect on her. Gradually, it helps transform how Precious looks at herself: Instead of feeling responsible for her parents' actions, she starts entertaining the notion that it is not her fault (137). Rain also imbues her with a sense of work ethic when she encourages her to keep writing and doing the emotional work required to heal. The word "push" is most often voiced in the novel by Rain, which underscores the parallel between *Push* and *The Color Purple* regarding the importance of mentors—who can potentially become focal points of new communities—since it is Shug who talks to Celie about her vision of the colour purple (223).

The work Precious is doing with Rain is later supplemented by attending various support groups and finding friends. In Precious's Harlem, the diffuse family structure that empowers Celie in the South is unattainable; instead, new forms of communities emerge. The members of her classroom, the support groups, and the women in the halfway house assist Precious, be it consciously or unwittingly. She assumes that her Blackness is the only reason she is a victim of incest, and she is revolted by her body that shows the signs of both her race and gender. Her concept of white privilege and attractiveness changes when during a support group meeting, she learns that white and conventionally attractive women can be victims of incest as well. After being isolated from her peers for the majority of her childhood and teenage years, she is validated when one of her friends—a blond woman—comments on the beauty of the name of Precious (143). Thus, being included in a community and being in a public place without having to feel ashamed have a healing effect on her, and by the end of the novel, she overcomes her victimized position.

Due to the influence of various discourses on gender, race, and motherhood, Precious at the beginning of the novel situates herself as an undesirable nonentity, worthless of her name. She defines herself through internalizing the hatred of mainstream society and her own family, which both sexually and financially exploits her. Through receiving help from her mentor, finding companionship, and deconstructing certain myths—such as being white equals having an easy life or being a teenage mother equals being an incompetent mother—she can extricate herself from the web of self-hatred. Thus, even though both Celie and Precious belong to the most marginalized groups of society and both are disconnected from their bodies and motherhood due to trauma, they gradually reappropriate motherhood after reclaiming bodily agency, but not with the help of institutions or through having a white saviour or a male companion. Instead, they find solace and strength with the help of Black female mentors and in more or less rhizomatically organized alternative communities, which become spaces of resistance.

I read these novels as political texts that interrogate the plight of young Black mothers. Both novelists were certainly criticized on several accounts. According to some critics, the utopia Walker created is unrealistic (Hite 103-04), whereas the descriptions of Black male brutality in *Push* do more harm than good (Bobo 332-33). Sapphire defended the overt visuality of her novel by asserting that the events described in graphic detail are necessary to convey accurately the reality of many girls whose lives resemble Precious's (Wilson and Sapphire 34-35). *The Color Purple*'s revolutionary nature lies in its references to slavery, whereas the subversive power of Sapphire's text lies in its overt and covert references to *The Color Purple*: Their structural and thematic similarities highlight how conditions of African American mothers have changed and remained the same even though mainstream society's views on race and gender transformed by the end of the twentieth century. An implicit aim that *Push* accomplishes is social critique. By alluding to *The Color Purple* on a multitude of textual levels, the novel argues that even though Black mothers like Precious have some access to aid from the state, essentially, they are just as marginalized as Walker's heroine. These cultural and intertextual allusions make up a structure in which *The Color Purple* shows that nothing has changed since slavery, and *Push* shows that nothing has changed since *The Color Purple*. The system that rests on the traumatic legacy of slavery can only be circumvented, as the novels suggest, by relying on the help of mentors and peers in alternative communities. Systemic race-, class-, and gender-based violence oppress these characters to such an extent that no institutional safety net can save them as people and as mothers because, as Martinot points out, the reason behind their subjugation is exactly the ideological needs of the system itself, which bell hooks has called white supremacist capitalist patriarchy (51). Ultimately, the spaces of resistance created by the mentors help the protagonists to accept their maternal subject positions and to transcend their vulnerability. These women, then, might later create communities and become mentors themselves, thus safeguarding the next generation of young Black women until the system changes.

Endnotes

1. The effects of motherhood on not only physical but also emotional/mental wellbeing are highlighted in the story Samuel tells Nettie about her mother: "Almost at once, she was pregnant a third time, though her mental health was no better. Every year thereafter, she was pregnant, every year she became weaker and more mentally unstable" (196).

   Nettie is similarly worried about Celie's mental health in connection with motherhood and abuse: "will you still have Tashi's honest and open spirit, I wonder, when we see you again? Or will years of childbearing and abuse from Mr. have destroyed it?" (308).

2. For details on and a historical overview of African American family structures that privilege short- and long-term care of children born to other Black women, see *All Our Kin: Strategies for Survival in a Black Community* (1974) by Carol D. Stack.

3. For a historical overview of Black families and a discussion of how their structures function as networks engendered despite slavery, see *The Black Family in Slavery and Freedom, 1750–1925* (1976) by Herbert Gutman.

Works Cited

Abbandonato, Linda. "'A View from 'Elsewhere': Subversive Sexuality and the Rewriting of the Heroine's Story in *The Color Purple*." *PMLA*, vol. 106, no. 5, 1991, pp. 1106–1115.

Abdullah, Melina. "Womanist Mothering: Loving and Raising the Revolution." *Western Journal of Black Studies,* vol 36, no. 1, 2012, pp. 57-67.

Bobo, Jacqueline. "Sifting Through the Controversy: Reading *The Color Purple*." *Callaloo*, vol. 39, 1989, pp. 332–42.

Collins, Patricia Hill. *Black Feminist Thought: Knowledge, Consciousness, and the Politics of Empowerment*. Routledge, 1990.

Collins, Patricia Hill. "Black Women and Motherhood." *Motherhood and Space: Configurations of the Maternal through Politics, Home, and The Body*, edited by Sarah Hardy and Caroline Wiedmer, Palgrave Macmillan, 2005, pp. 149-59.

Dagbovie-Mullins, Sika A. "From Living to Eat to Writing to Live: Metaphors of Consumption and Production in Sapphire's *Push*." *African American Review*, vol. 2, 2011, pp. 435-52.

Deleuze, Gilles, and Félix Guattari. *A Thousand Plateaus: Capitalism and Schizophrenia*. University of Minnesota Press, 1987.

Fulton, DoVeanna, S. "Looking for 'the Alternative[s]:' Locating Sapphire's *Push* in African American Literary Tradition through Literacy and Orality." *Sapphire's Literary Breakthrough. Erotic Literacies, Feminist Pedagogies, Environmental Justice Perspectives*, edited by Elizabeth McNeil, et al., Palgrave Macmillan, 2012, pp. 161-70.

Gutman, Herbert. *The Black Family in Slavery and Freedom, 1750–1925*. Random House, 1976.

Hite, Molly. "Romance, Marginality, Matrilineage: *The Color Purple*." *The Other Side of the Story: Structures and Strategies of Contemporary Feminist Narratives*, edited by Molly Hite, Cornell University Press, 1989, pp. 103-26.

hooks, bell. *Feminist Theory: From Margin to Center*. South End Press, 1984.

Lundquist, Caroline. "Being Torn: Toward a Phenomenology of Unwanted Pregnancy." *Hypatia*, vol. 23, no. 3, 2008, pp. 136-55.

Martinot, Steven. "Motherhood and the Invention of Race." *Hypatia*, vol. 22, no. 2, 2007, pp. 79-97.

McNeil, Elizabeth. "Un-'Freak'ing Black Female Selfhood: Grotesque-Erotic Agency and Ecofeminist Unity in Sapphire's *Push*." *MELUS*, vol. 37, no. 4, 2012, pp. 11-30.

Michlin, Monica. "Narrative as Empowerment: *Push* and the Signifying on Prior African-American Novels on Incest." *Études Anglaises*, vol. 2, no. 2, 2006, pp. 170-85.

Morrison, Toni. *Playing in the Dark: Whiteness and the Literary Imagination*. Vintage, 1993.

Rich, Adrienne. *Of Woman Born: Motherhood As Experience and Institution*. Norton, 1976.

Sapphire. *Push: A Novel*. Vintage, 1996.

Schneider, Dorothy, and Carl J. Schneider. *Slavery in America*. Facts on File, 2007.

Spillers, Hortense J. "Mama's Baby, Papa's Maybe: An American Grammar Book." *Diacritics,* vol. 17, no. 2, 1987, pp. 64-81.

Stack, Carol D. *All Our Kin: Strategies for Survival in a Black Community*. Harper and Row, 1974.

Walker, Alice. *The Color Purple*. Pocket Books, 1982.

Wilson, Marq, and Sapphire. "'A Push out of Chaos': An Interview with Sapphire." *MELUS*, vol. 37, no. 4, 2012, pp. 31–39.

Chapter 4

The Ripple Effect of Mothering in a Global Community: From Bloomington to Bogotá

Silvia Rivera-Largacha and Angela N. Castañeda

Introduction

Each day, hundreds of thousands of women around the world experience the transformative rite of passage that is giving birth. We know that birth marks not only a mother but also an entire community, as new identities and sociocultural networks are formed and expanded. In this chapter, we explore the ripple effects of one birth as well as the role that friendship plays in connecting and impacting global mothering communities. To assist this exploration, we follow the ripple effects of birth from one community to another—taking us across international borders from Bloomington, Indiana, to Bogotá, Colombia.

By looking at new mothers and the active process of becoming mothers, our work seeks to privilege "maternal bodies in the production of new selves" (Longhurst 4). We find this period in a woman's life as a particularly useful time for women to reflect and connect via corporeal and social status fluidity associated with what it means to become a mother. This analysis includes a relational awareness of mothering as both complicated and active as well as shaped and defined by context (Jeremiah 24). We use autoethnography to examine the intersections of mothering across international borders and to unpack how our mothering experiences have fostered a deeper friendship and stronger global mothering community.

Our work began in Bloomington, Indiana, where we traced the impact of a nonprofit organization that strives to empower mothers by providing safe spaces and opportunities for community building. Through her first birth experience in 2012, Rivera-Largacha unpacked the role this mothering community had on her initiation into motherhood and her subsequent friendship with Castañeda. Following her return to her native Colombia, Rivera-Largacha continued to weave a positive and humanistic approach to childbirth by increasing academic and community-based support for partoshumanizados, or humanized births. Four years later, both authors reunited in March 2016 after Rivera-Largacha organized, and Castañeda presented her work at, the first collaborative conference at the Universidad del Rosario on humanized birth in Colombia. By following the ripple effect of birth, our work demonstrates the power of mothering to weave ties of cooperation and international friendship that foster the strengthening of movements and policies that promote the defense of women's rights in childbirth.

The Roots of a Birth Community: Bloomington

Established in 1994, Bloomington Area Birth Services (BABS) began as a group of five mothers who were looking for additional childbirth support and education. From this core group of women, a wave of resources emerged. BABS was incorporated as a non-profit in 2004 with a mission "to improve the lives of mothers and babies by increasing breastfeeding rates, treating perinatal mood and anxiety disorders, providing new families with education and resources, and maintaining a safe place where families can gather for mutual support" (Clarke). BABS extended its mission beyond childbirth education and prenatal yoga to include a retail shop with books, cloth diapers, and maternity clothes as well as a lending library, volunteer and community-based doula programs, lactation services, a milk-donor station, toddler playgroups, and support groups for new moms, fathers, siblings, grandparents, and women interested in VBACs (vaginal birth after a caesarean). BABS sustained its growth through program fees, most of which were based on reasonable prices and a sliding pay scale targeted at low-income populations, individual donations, grants, annual fundraisers, and retail sales.

Both of us, Castañeda and Rivera-Largacha, received services at BABS, including prenatal education, perinatal yoga, exercise, as well as postpartum support. Castañeda also served on the board of directors for BABS from 2010 to 2012 and was trained and certified as a postpartum and birth doula working with the BABS community. Through our varied embodied experiences of mothering facilitated at BABS, we came to recognize how this organization was contributing to the production and acceptance of mothering as an active process. In essence, BABS cultivated new opportunities for the gendered performance of mothering or the "set of repeated citational and bodily acts that produce the appearance of the 'natural' and the 'true'" (Longhurst 9). Understanding maternal performativity as an active process is already a progressive notion when framed by the traditional Western understanding of a mother as passive, but it can also be understood as subversive or an act of resistance (Jeremiah 21). Drawing upon the work of sociocultural geographer Robyn Longhurst, the programming at BABS sought to emphasize the maternal body as "what surely must be one of, if not the, most important of all bodies—bodies that conceive, give birth, and nurture other bodies" and as "constructed differently through different social and cultural networks" (2-3). The work of BABS included the construction of important social and cultural networks for new mothers.

In 2013, at the height of BABS outreach, when it was serving over eight hundred families annually, it inaugurated its Blooming Families program, partially funded by the Indiana State Department of Health, which included community-based doulas to provide families with wrap-around services focused on pregnancy, birth, postpartum, and breastfeeding (Clarke). Despite its diverse programming and positive outcomes, and following an intense fundraising effort, BABS was forced to close its doors in the fall of 2015 due to financial difficulties. The research for this project was collected at the height of BABS's popularity, and it documents the importance and far-reaching impact of celebrating the maternal body in the community.

The First Waves of the Ripple: A Birth Story

Rivera-Largacha is a scholar at a medical school and a member of a small minority of Colombians with access to good quality healthcare, provided predominantly by private corporations. She lives in Bogotá, Colombia. During the first trimester of her first pregnancy, Rivera-Largacha experienced the membership benefits of friendship and solidarity of the BABS community. BABS is a community grounded in the strength of women supporting women. Membership in BABS made her realize the limited access most women in her home country of Colombia have to quality maternal healthcare. Thus, during her second pregnancy in 2014, her status did not ensure easy access to the same type of quality healthy birth options she had had with her first pregnancy. In Colombia, she did not have a place where information about pregnancy, childbirth, and parenting could be accessed or performed with such fluidity. Normally her conversations with her friends who were pregnant or had children were limited. Although new parents in Bogotá have access to the literature and technical information surrounding birth, there is not a formal social space to exchange experiences, express questions, and share feelings in the construction of a lived community sharing vivid knowledge. In Colombia, parenthood is still a very private experience and sometimes a lonely experience.

As she started this new chapter of her life, she realized that the inequalities in health services in her country were especially problematic for maternal healthcare. While she recognized that her gynecologist was a great physician who had returned to her obstetric practice after time off to raise her children, Rivera-Largacha soon learned from her the difficult working conditions for care providers hoping for more humanized care with births. During her third month of pregnancy, she moved to Bloomington, Indiana, and became an invited scholar at the Karl Schuessler Institute of Social Research (KSISR) at Indiana University. As she tried to locate opportunities for prenatal exercise, she also tried to fulfill her basic expectation—have physical support—so she could have an active and healthy pregnancy and give birth to her baby boy. She would find much of what she was searching for at BABS.

After passing through the doors of BABS, Rivera-Largacha was surprised by the immediate display of care and empathy she received from virtual strangers upon her first moments in this space. Even the architecture of the space was conceived to welcome and fulfill the varied needs of a new mother. In particular, there was a living room where people could congregate before or after the different classes, a kitchen to prepare coffee, tea, and snacks, and a bookshelf with literature related to pregnancy, birth, and parenting. At the entrance, there was a small boutique with various pregnancy, baby, and lactation accessories as well as a corner with second-hand pregnancy clothes for sale. It was in this space at BABS that she found the yoga classes she was looking for; in the end, she gained a community and so much more, including but not limited to prenatal education, a celebratory birth dance class, a doula, a new mom's group, and lactation support.

As she became a regular attendee at BABS, Rivera-Largacha found herself becoming closer to this community—a community that showed a sincere interest in the experience she was having with her growing family. In particular, prenatal yoga classes became a special space of enjoyment, as she could focus on caring for her body and communicating with her baby boy through exercise and meditation. At the prenatal yoga classes, she met Polina Reinhold, a Russian language teacher, who like Rivera-Largacha was living temporarily in Bloomington. Reinhold invited Rivera-Largacha to join her in Dancing for Birth classes designed for perinatal support and education. In these classes, Rivera-Largacha experienced a whole new way to embody notions of femininity, pregnancy, and motherhood. Dancing for Birth classes were special moments where pregnant women and new mothers were brought together to dance in a circle. Rivera-Largacha found that dancing in a circle became a way of visualizing bodies in their transformation process—in particular, maternal bodies. The narrative presented by the instructors created a context of support and complicity where each body was seen as a space of beauty and strength. For pregnant mothers dancing with new mothers, listening to their birth stories and experiences of postpartum became valuable information used to boost confidence and agency during pregnancy, birth, and postpartum. Rivera-Largacha used the tools fostered by her new community to help ease her transition to motherhood via the unmedicated vaginal birth of her son in 2012.

In a social context marked by the obsession with efficiency and rivalry and by a fixation with the objectification of women's bodies,

BABS's services were grounded in a resistance narrative, in which intuition, dissimilar processes, and cooperation between women and families were emphasized and strengthened. Following her son's birth, Rivera-Largacha leaned on the BABS community and the strength of other new mothers to walk with her. Castañeda had been part of a similar community after the birth of her son, and it was this mutual connection and shared academic interests that brought us together as coauthors. BABS could weave people together, like strands of fine string, into a strong piece of colorful tapestry. BABS united our energies and connected us on multiple levels as scholars and mothers. Additionally, Castañeda had a unique history with Rivera-Largacha's country, having lived there when she was younger—a link that made the friendship more special and the bond even stronger. Together, we shared experiences as mothers of sons, an invested interest in embodied knowledge as scholars, and a commitment to humanized birth as reproductive justice advocates.

Colombia is a country where obstetric healthcare has been profoundly marked by medicalization, which has led to the silence of women's voices. In Colombia, the number of caesarean sections has been on the rise, increasing 20.8 per cent from 27.4 per cent from 1990 to 2014 (Betrán et al.). This increase has begun to generate discussion among healthcare users, providers, and administrators as well as among activists, politicians, and other social actors. Most recently, conversations have gradually emerged about the overmedicalization of birth among small circles of obstetricians. For example, the Colombian Gynecological Federation highlighted the problematic caesarean section increase in the *Colombian Journal of Obstetrics and Gynecology*: "The rate of caesarean sections in the country has been in constant increase from 1998 until 2013, despite a decrease in the total number of births and birth rate and is above the standards or levels recommended by international organizations" (Rubio-Romero 147). However, this article does not identify the social dynamics that produce this outcome, nor does it propose changes to address this situation. Another more recent article published in the same journal in 2017 further reflected on the treatment of mothers: "Health services all over the world have been changing their practices and adapting their organizations to provide more humanized treatment in maternal care" (Cáceres-Manrique 129). In this article, humanized birth is recognized as clinical services offered to give clear information concerning all medical processes as well as the reasons for their use, risks, and benefits.

The inequity in access to health services and the particular disadvantages for women from vulnerable populations—such as adolescents, high-risk pregnancies, or mothers of low socioeconomic conditions—have not yet been studied in Colombia. In 2012, Jorge Caballero, a Colombian film director, presented a documentary about this situation entitled *Nacer: Diario de Maternidad (Born: Maternity Diary)*. As he filmed in hospitals in Bogotá, he captured the essence of these inequalities. His work analyzed the deep roots of machismo, vulnerability, and the violence rooted in Colombia's past. The documentary is aptly described as follows: "Case by case, birth by birth, social reality is revealed with each situation. Wait, meet, love, defend, accept and resist, are the verbs that make up this demystifying picture of hospital births. *Nacer: Diario de Maternidad* is the direct portrait of several lives in six days that reflects an essential part of a country" (Caballero). By looking through the lens of birth, this documentary acts as a mirror to reflect the inequalities and the violence of the larger Colombian society, especially for its most vulnerable populations; there are regional and ethnic disparities among Indigenous and Afro-Colombian communities, and "although humanized childbirth has been defined and appears in documents and care guidelines of international organizations proclaiming its application in every pregnant patient during prenatal follow-up, labour and delivery, it does not benefit all women equally" (Cáceres-Manrique 128-29). Although formal research is lacking on this subject, it is evident that the push towards humanized birth in Colombia is still limited, touching only a small portion of the population from privileged socioeconomic communities.

Growing a Global Maternal Community

Upon her return to Bogotá, Rivera-Largacha became pregnant with her second child and began to realize the privileged experiences she previously had in the Bloomington birth community. In Colombia, midwifery does not exist as a profession. For example, there are no midwifery schools or postgraduate programs for obstetric nurses. Besides, midwifery is restricted to the inherited knowledge learned from traditional healers mostly in Afro-Colombian, Indigenous, and rural communities. In this context, urban pregnancies and births are attended in their great majority by obstetricians or physicians in hospitals. In these conditions, the medicalization of birth is hegemonic.

Recently, a small urban movement is growing around the idea of home birth in Colombia. Some rural and ethnic midwives are starting to work in urban spaces, and we also find the appearance of urban midwives, who are mostly professionals from different areas who have apprenticed with traditional midwives. Nonetheless, midwifery practices are not recognized by official health services, and midwives work without any legislative regulation. In this context, physicians and obstetricians do not trust this urban midwifery movement. They are also suspicious about the presence of doulas at birth. Although doula advocacy has increased, obstetricians associate and even confuse doulas with the work of urban midwives (de Vries and de Vries); in most hospitals in Bogotá, doulas are not allowed to support during childbirth (Castañeda and Searcy 124-39).

Given these circumstances, Rivera-Largacha found herself without many options for healthcare outside the hospital services for her second pregnancy. When she tried to hire a doula, she was informed that the hospital where she was going to give birth allowed only two people to support a woman during childbirth: two trained nurses who were certified by the hospital to work as acompañantes de parto, or childbirth supporters. Despite these conditions, Rivera-Largacha and her family had a healthy pregnancy, delivery, and postpartum period for their second child; that being said, she felt that she had missed the social support she had experienced in Bloomington. This experience of transitioning to a mother of two was more private and lonelier, as is commonly the case in Colombia.

Motivated by her personal experiences, Rivera-Largacha started to build a research group focused on maternity with her friends Claudia Cortés, an anthropologist, who was finishing her PhD thesis on public health, and one of her students, Jenny Muñoz, a bacteriologist specializing in public health management. Muñoz was working with vulnerable communities in two isolated and unequal territories in Colombia: Chocó, where she became a midwife apprentice, and Cesar. And like Rivera-Largacha, Cortés, a scholar studying sexual and reproductive health, was also navigating the new world of motherhood with the birth of her daughter in 2011.

In March 2016, Cortés, Muñoz, and Rivera-Largacha galvanized global support for the first collaborative conference on partos humanizados, or humanized birth, in Colombia. The timing of this conference was critical given Colombia's decades-long violent past and attempts at peace negotiations between the government and the Revolutionary Armed Forces of Colombia. Rivera-Largacha sought to build upon her embodied and scholarly experiences with mothering, both in Bloomington and Bogotá, by reviewing the practices surrounding pregnancy, childbirth, postpartum, and parenting in her home country. At the core of this gathering was the belief that pregnancy, childbirth, and the first months of parenting are sacred spaces that offer windows into understanding complex sociocultural dynamics. The conference also gave space to a discussion on how pregnant women, new mothers, and their children are cared for during the perinatal period and how this treatment reveals the types of social bonds that exist and are valued in a particular context. As such, this conference became a place to analyze how birth in Colombia was one of many spaces in which violence had marked the lives of women, children, and a larger national community. As a renowned, North American midwife Ina May Gaskin aptly writes, "The way a culture treats women in birth is a good indicator of how well women and their contributions to society are valued and honored" (6).

At the conference, new alliances were built and knowledge was shared, as participants from across Colombia and beyond were brought together. Though originally planned as a one-day event, the conference became a three-day meeting including a variety of groups and diverse public participation. There were undergraduates from different disciplines, including medical students as well as gynecologists, midwives, doulas, anthropologists, sociologists, lawyers, and reproductive scholars in attendance. Many organizations presented on their valuable community-based programs.[1] The presence of ASOREDIPARCHOCO was especially significant at the conference. This association is constituted by people from Indigenous and Afro-Colombian communities who are working to recover and preserve their ancestral traditions around pregnancy, birth, breastfeeding, and childcare through an intercultural conversation with the formal health services offered by the Colombian state. The midwives representing the

Chocó region, ten women and one man, made the nearly fifteen-hour journey by bus to attend the conference. Chocó is a region characterized by its isolation and the social inequalities affecting marginalized communities mostly populated by Indigenous and Afro-Colombian people; it was, therefore, important to hear these voices at the conference as well as support their work to preserve their knowledge and defend the rights of their people. In the Chocó region, health services are rare and inefficient; thus, midwives and traditional healers are the healthcare providers and human rights defenders.

Although the purpose of the conference was to focus on birth conditions within Colombia, it included testimonials from two international scholars, Castañeda and Aleida Marroquín, a gynecologist and obstetrician working on humanized birth in her home country of El Salvador. Reflecting on her life, Castañeda noted that two transformative experiences marked her identity. The first happened over twenty years ago when she first stepped foot on Colombian soil as a young woman on the verge of entering adulthood and forming her identity as Latina, Mexican American, and citizen of the Americas. The second life-altering experience was her entrance to motherhood nearly ten years ago with the birth of her first child. Thus, it seemed only fitting that her long-awaited return to Colombia would bridge both of these transformative experiences, as she returned with her own family to engage in discussions on the importance of humanized birth. At the conference, Castañeda presented her paper, "Lazos entre Mujeres: el papel de la doula en el parto humanizado," which focused on the role of BABS, and doulas in particular, in humanized birth. Her work as a board member and doula in the BABS community enabled her to emphasize the importance of building spaces that respect the sacred liminal space associated with childbirth as well as the construction of new models of maternal bodies. This work privileges informed decision-making options for all women during their pregnancy, birth, and postpartum, thus crafting spaces for an increased agency for women and new families.

Marroquín, who worked as an obstetrician with the nongovernmental organization Doctors Without Borders, spent two years in the Chocó region of Colombia learning from midwives and traditional healers on Chocó approaches to motherhood and mothering practices. At the conference, she shared her experiences as a Western-trained obstetrician trying to support humanized birth professionally in an environment deemed resistant to change. El Salvador, like Colombia, is a country whose citizens suffer from the effects of war, which contributes to a cultural context that naturalizes violence against women and, thus, leads to negative and even violent birth experiences. The years she spent working with women giving birth in vulnerable communities and extreme conditions made her realize the importance of empowering women to participate in the birthing process. The midwives from the Chocó region who were in the public during her presentation listened to the description Marroquín shared about her cooperative work with the midwives, women, and the people of different vulnerable communities including those from Chocó. As Marroquin finished her presentation, one midwife from this region stood up and said, "You should come back, madam. We need people like you in our community."

From Bloomington to Bogotá, as well as passing through El Salvador and different regions within Colombia, the social ties and the emotional connections surrounding birth became the foundation for a multiplicity of projects offering new options to women in the care of their sexual and reproductive health and during their transition to motherhood. We believe an analysis of the social construction of the body is the first step in understanding the construction of a larger more peaceful social body. It is also our hope that researching this area can lead us to understand social ties as forms of interaction where we find the body as the first territory of inscription for social experiences and interactions. Ultimately, the research and experiences helped to reposition mothers and the act of mothering by recognizing scenarios for new forms of care and relationship building to claim maternal bodies as territories of peace.

Conclusion: Creating Cascades of Change

Birth workers and care providers often describe the "cascade of interventions" that women are faced with when their pregnancies or births are overmedicalized. What if instead we focused on the cascade of positive change? In this chapter, we traced the reverberations from birth and lifecycle of an organization as well as the subsequent friendships that developed. Today, we continue to see the ever-changing and expanding ripple effects of birth in both communities: Bloomington and Bogotá.

Bloomington

The seeds that were planted in Bloomington by BABS are still growing. While Bloomington saw the closure of BABS in 2015, the birth community was reborn that same year as the All-Options Pregnancy Resource Center—a nonprofit that is led by self-described "reproductive justice advocates" who support "pregnancy, parenting, adoption, and abortion, all under one roof" (Nathan). Described as "open-hearted and open-minded," the type of support offered at All-Options seeks to serve as an alternative to the polarized debate surrounding pregnancy in the United States (Barbato). In addition to offering "unbiased and nonjudgmental peer counseling" and cultivating volunteers from the local community, All-Options also offers "free pregnancy tests, concrete resources like diapers and baby items, and referrals to the care and resources people need—whether that includes birthing support, abortion funding, adoption information, contraceptives, insurance coverage, child care, or all of the above" (Nathman). Instead of marginalizing women during liminal periods of their reproductive life histories, All-Options seeks to continue the work begun by BABS through programming that not only reintegrates but also welcomes women to a community regardless of their new identity formed from birth, adoption, abortion, or miscarriage.

Bogotá

After the 2016 conference in Bogotá, the social interest in the subject of obstetric violence and the humanization of maternal healthcare has increased. Five months after the closing of the 2016 conference, the conversations and opportunities for more positive work continued when Rivera-Largacha invited Susana Bueno, an obstetrician in Bogotá, to a public talk about her experience with humanized birth in her professional practice. Bueno began her talk wearing a white lab coat and described her first years of practice as a physician and obstetrician. She discussed the naturalization of clinical practices, in which health providers treated women in a purely technical way during childbirth, discounted or dismissed patient requests, and avoided any questioning of their medical practices. She eventually began to listen to the women she was taking care of and quickly learned that women were asking to have the freedom to move during childbirth, to stay in different positions, and to have the company and support from their partner, their relatives, or a doula; they were asking to have a vaginal birth after a caesarean section and for alternatives to pain management. In general, they were asking to have an appropriate amount of input into their own healthcare decisions and for more support during childbirth. Bueno realized that the answers to these particular requests were hard to find inside the system that shaped her as a physician. She realized it was time for her to open her mind and search for safe and practical ways to help her patients with these requests inside a system resistant to change. Bueno participated in several doula training programs to reconnect with the emotional aspects of the birthing process and travelled to rural communities across Colombia that are working to preserve their midwifery traditions. Through these experiences, in addition to her research on best practices during the perinatal period, Bueno and Rivera-Largacha have found a common cause that not only has strengthened their friendship but has also led to the creation of an academic research cooperative.

Just as the 2016 conference was a space that brought different groups together, it also created many new initiatives through the construction of innovative ties of cooperation. Moreover, it awakened the interest of politicians, as two women senators are currently proposing two new laws concerning humanization in childbirth and the prevention of obstetric violence. In this context, healthcare providers, especially gynecologists and obstetricians from the Federación Colombiana de Ginecobstetricia (FECOLSOG), are starting to discuss these subjects, as they recently created a working group dedicated to them. A key active participant in this newly formed group is Susana Bueno, who is energizing the dialogue by bridging the work of academics, paediatricians, and birth community workers, including doulas, midwives, and lactation consultants. Together, Bueno and Rivera-Largacha are creating strong collaborative projects that draw upon their friendship and a mutual passion to change the conditions of health for women in Colombia.

Each day, hundreds of thousands of women around the world experience the transformative rite of passage that is the birthing process. We know that birth marks not only a mother but an entire community, as new identities and sociocultural networks are formed and existing ones expanded. The energies that were involved in the creation of BABS, a single nonprofit organization, went on to influence other areas of our lives and have since sustained the community of mothers and expanded our circle of friends. From this friendship, we have traced ever-expanding circles of hope, change, and strength among mothers and thus empowered more women to form communities to promote and defend women's and motherhood rights.

Endnotes

1. These organizations include the Asociación de la red interétnica de parteras y parteros del departamento del Chocó ASOREDIPARCHOCO, Observatorio de Salud Sexual y Reproductiva, Observatorio de Violencia Obstétrica–OVO (Corporación Mujeres Bachué), Women's Link Worldwide, Asociación Parir, Corporación Acunado, and Camino Claro (the Association of the inter-ethnic network of midwives and midwives of the department of Chocó ASOREDIPARCHOCO, Observatory of Sexual and Reproductive Health, Observatory of Obstetric Violence–OVO (Bachué Women's Corporation), Women's Link Worldwide, Parir Association Accunado Society, and Clear Path).

Works Cited

Barbato, Lauren. "Indiana's All-Options Pregnancy Resource Center Finally Offers Women The 'Options' They Actually Need." *Bustle*, 12 May 2015. www.bustle.com/articles/79838-indianas-all-options-pregnancy-resource-center-finally-offers-women-the-options-they-actually-need. Accessed 13 Feb. 2022.

Betrán Ana Pilar, et al. "The Increasing Trend in Caesarean Section Rates: Global, Regional and National Estimates: 1990-2014." *PLoS ONE*, vol. 11, no. 2, 2016, p. e0148343.

Caballero, Jorge. *Nacer, diario de maternidad*. Gusano Films, Colombia, 2012, http://www.gusano.org/project/nacer/. Accessed 13 Feb. 2022.

Cáceres-Manrique, Flor de María, and Giselly Mayerly Nieves-Cuervo. "Atención humanizada el parto: Diferencial según condición clínica y social de la materna." *Revista Colombiana de*

Obstetricia y Ginecología, vol. 68, no. 2, 2017, pp. 128-34.

Castañeda, Angela N., and Julie Johnson Searcy. "My Role is to Walk the Tightrope: Doulas and Intimacy." *Doulas and Intimate Labour: Boundaries, Bodies and Birth*, edited by Angela N Castañeda, Demeter Press, 2015, pp. 124-39.

Clarke, Mandy. "Bloomington Area Birth Services Now Helping 800 Local Families." *Bloom Magazine*, 2013, www.magbloom.com/2013/09/bloomington-area-birth-services-now-helping-800-local-families/. Accessed 13 Feb. 2022.

Gaskin, Ina May. *Birth Matters: A Midwife's Manifesta*. Seven Stories Press, 2011.

Integrantes del Consenso de la Federación Colombiana de Obstetricia y Ginecología (Fecolsog) y la Federación Colombiana de Perinatología (Fecopen). "Racionalización del uso de la cesárea en Colombia. Consenso de la Federación Colombiana de Obstetricia y Ginecología (Fecolsog) y la Federación Colombiana de Perinatología (Fecopen)." *Revista Colombiana de Obstetricia y Ginecología*, vol. 65, no. 2, 2014, pp. 139-51.

Jeremiah, Emily. "Motherhood to Mothering and Beyond: Maternity in Recent Feminist Thought." *Journal of the Motherhood Initiative for Research and Community Involvement*, vol. 8, no. 1, 2006, pp. 21-33.

Longhurst, Robyn. *Maternities: Gender, Bodies and Space*. Routledge, 2012.

Nathman, Avital Normal. "This New Pregnancy Center will be the First of its Kind." *Cosmopolitan*, 19 Sept. 2014, www.cosmopolitan.com/lifestyle/news/a31285/backline-pregnancy-resource-center/. Accessed 13 Feb. 2022.

Norena-Herrera, Camilo, et al. "Inequidad en la utilización de servicios de salud reproductiva en Colombia en mujeres indígenas y afrodescendientes." *Cadernos de Saúde Pública*, vol. 31, no. 12, 2015, pp. 2635-48.

Rubio-Romero, Jorge Andrés, et al. "Consensus for the Rationalization of Cesarean Section Use in Colombia. Federación colombiana de Obstetricia y Ginecología (FecOlsOG) and Federacón colombiana de Perinatología (FecOPen). Bogotá, 2014." *Revista Colombiana de Obstetricia y Ginecología*, vol. 65, no. 2, 2014, pp. 139-51.

Stevens, Jeni, Hannah Dahlen, et al. "Midwives' and Doulas' Perspectives of the Role of the Doula in Australia: A Qualitative Study." *Midwifery*, vol. 27, no. 4, 2011, pp. 509-16.

United States Census Bureau. "Quick Facts." *Census*, www.census.gov/quickfacts/fact/table/bloomingtoncityindiana/LND110210. Accessed 13 Feb. 2022.

Vries, Charlotte A. de, and Raymond G. de Vries. "Childbirth Education in the 21st Century: An Immodest Proposal." *The Journal of Perinatal Education*, vol. 16, no. 4, 2007, pp. 38-48.

Chapter 5

Film as Invitational Rhetoric: Transcending Motherhood Narratives through Community in *20th Century Women*

Rachel D. Davidson and Catherine A. Dobris

Principal: Now, Jamie, you can't just keep skipping school and making excuses.

Dorothea: Well wait a minute, why not? Why can't he just skip school if he has a legitimate need to be away?

Principal: Well, then I need a legitimate real note from you...

Dorothea: Okay.

Principal: With your real signature [handing Dorothea, a forged school note]

Dorothea (turning to face Jamie): Wow, how did you forge my signature so well?

Set in the late 1970s, Mike Mills's film *20th Century Women* (2016) positions single mother, Dorothea Fields, as both narrator and subject of a vision that extends parenting definitions beyond a singular, maternal figure while transgressing the binary boundaries of good-bad mothering. When fifty-five-year-old Dorothea struggles to connect with her fifteen-year-old son, Jamie, she cajoles friends and acquaintances to assist in parenting her son. In the process, viewers are invited to enter an alternate parenting reality in which the norms of Western motherhood are challenged in a complex counternarrative to traditional media portrayals of parenting. As the above exchange between Dorothea and Jamie's high school principal illustrates, conventional power hierarchies are questioned and boundaries between parent and child remain fluid throughout the film. We are invited to evaluate and reevaluate what it means to be a good mother by following a coming-of-age story that synthesizes traditional and nontraditional approaches to parenting.

Scholarly explorations of motherhood have examined the manifestations of patriarchal motherhood in public discourse. For example, scholars explore mediated representations of parenting and reveal the complicated relationships between resistance to, and reinforcement of, patriarchal motherhood (Boser; Davidson and Stache; Davidson and Dobris, et al.; Podnieks). Heather Hayden and Sara Hundley further suggest the following: "Something new is taking place on the contemporary media landscape. That is, on television, movie screens, and the Internet maternal images are deviating from the good/bad binary, providing more nuanced portraits of mothers and mothering" (2). *20th Century Women* functions, thus, as an expression of this "new... contemporary media landscape" (Hayden and Hundley 2), and the current investigation looks to this text and its "potential to embody contradictions—not to present an either/or dichotomy but a both/and perspective" (5). When this occurs, audiences are invited to enter a "both/and" mindset on mothering by expanding their frame of reference on contemporary parenting ideals. This process facilitates a multifaceted view of parenting for the audience. It also allows the audience to experience a range of parenting options not usually permitted in mainstream media portrayals of mothering. Analysis of these options reveals the theoretical assumptions inherent in the artifact.

In her paradigmatic work on mothering archetypes, Adrienne Rich (1986) distinguishes between two visions of motherhood deep-rooted in public culture. She identifies prototypical themes in contemporary cultural expressions: "relationally empowered mothering," which is "the potential relationship of any woman to her powers of reproduction and to children" (13) and "patriarchal motherhood ... which aims at ensuring that that potential—and all women—shall remain under male control" (13). Some research suggests that relationally empowered mothering is socially constructed to increase the liberating possibilities of mothering practices. Andrea O'Reilly describes this as a process to "mother against motherhood" (161). The current chapter explores how *20th Century Women* "mothers against motherhood" by both revealing and resisting patriarchal principles that co-construct a transcendent narrative of mothering. The use of invitational rhetoric as a theoretical framework reveals how *20th Century Women* offers a liberated model of mothering through its themes of community and friendship. In this vein, *20th Century Women* invites viewers to see motherhood more broadly via transcendent themes demonstrated by a community of pseudo-parents whose childrearing choices reimagine parenting as more than mother's work and transgress the socially constructed dichotomy of good-bad mothering. Rich's conception of "relationally empowered mothering" (13) is realized in both the viewing and subsequent analysis of the film.

Invitational Rhetoric

Invitational rhetoric is an alternative theory of rhetoric. It resists a "rhetoric of patriarchy" (Foss and Griffin 4) and embraces "rhetoric built on the principles of equality, immanent value, and self-determination rather than on an attempt to control others through persuasive strategies designed to effect change" (4-5). There are two primary components of invitational rhetoric: first, "offering perspectives" and, second, creating "an atmosphere in which audience members' perspectives also can be offered" (10). Offering perspectives "occurs not through persuasive argument but through offering—the giving of expression to a perspective without advocating its support or seeking its acceptance" (7). In the study, we use the "offering perspectives" concept as an analytical tool to conceptualize how "audience members' perspectives" help to create a complex mothering narrative in *20th Century Women*. By so doing, we contribute to the necessary scholarly work that locates and promotes liberated models of mothering through the interrogation of contemporary popular artifacts.

Feminist academic analyses of mediated cultural artifacts, such as film, are facilitated by offering perspectives for four reasons. First, film as a rhetorical artifact represents a narrative that meets many of the preconditions of invitational rhetoric. Film "constitutes an invitation to the audience to enter the rhetor's world and to see it as the rhetor does" (Foss and Griffin 5). Sonia K. Foss and Cindy L. Griffin assert that when a rhetor offers their viewpoint, "a story is not told as a means of supporting or achieving some other end but as an end in itself—simply offering the perspective the story represents" (7). Furthermore, offering perspectives can include "extending one another's ideas, thinking critically about all the ideas offered, and coming to an understanding of the subject" as well as "offering additional ways of thinking about the subject" (8). A film can be read, then, as an end product that "constitutes an invitation" to think critically about an issue. Second, as argued by Foss and Griffin, offering "can occur whether or not an audience chooses to join with a rhetor in a process of discovery and understanding" (10). Thus, offering perspectives is a useful way to observe a public artifact, even when the audience reception of that artifact is unavailable. Third, Foss and Griffin postulate that offering "may be seen in the nonverbal realm ... in all of the symbolic choices rhetors make that reveal their perspectives" (9). The symbolic choices made in a film narrative, both verbal and nonverbal, are accessible units of analysis available for scholars to interrogate. Finally, since invitational rhetoric is rooted in feminist principles, it is a suitable framework to help reveal the ways in which mediated texts, such as film, may offer alternatives to audience members who wish to challenge precepts of patriarchal motherhood.

20th Century Women: The Rhetorical Artifact

Set in 1979 Santa Barbara, California, *20th Century Women* portrays the strained relationship between Dorothea and her son, Jamie, and their community of friends. The central storyline follows Dorothea and Jamie as they navigate the difficult terrain of a son coming of age and a mother struggling to relate and adapt to the evolving sociopolitical and cultural scenes that animate their relationship. Throughout the film, Dorothea seeks parenting counsel from her boarding house tenants, Abbie and William, as well as from Jamie's best friend, seventeen-year-old Julie. A unique narrative develops for each member of this community in which their backstories emerge as grounding for their contributions to Jamie's childrearing. More importantly, the narrative for each member purposefully intersects with an aspect of Dorothea's parenting of her son.

Dorothea and Jamie take turns narrating the film from various points in the future and providing meta-analyses of their places in 1970s culture. In many respects, the character of Dorothea represents a significant departure from traditional values regarding, for example, sexuality and recreational drug use; but in other respects, she harkens back to mid-twentieth-century cultural mores. She frequently references older music and vintage films, admires classic automobiles and historic homes, and insists that men should still court women in conventionally gendered relational roles. As the film evolves, it becomes harder to predict whether Dorothea's behaviours—whether traditional or dissident—are within her latitude of acceptance. Her efforts to relate to her son throughout the film run parallel to her attempts to reconcile modern culture, music, and the second wave of feminism with some of her long-established expectations and assumptions.

In contrast, on the cusp of the twenty-first-century, Jamie represents contemporary culture. He hangs out with his counterculture friends and listens to The Talking Heads, David Bowie, as well as cutting-edge punk rock groups, such as The Raincoats and Germs. A typical teenager in some respects, Jamie challenges his mother's conservative viewpoint that is locked in her 1930s Depression-era childhood. He sees her views as antiquated and irrelevant to contemporary life issues. Jamie spends afternoons skateboarding with friends and seeks to embrace some tenets of contemporary feminism by reading the popular feminist text, *Our Bodies, Our Selves*, provided by Abbie. In this way, he hopes to understand and appreciate women better. His interests, past-times, and conversations throughout the film, highlight other key facets of the late 1970s to early 1980s.

Although Jamie's characterization reflects the time in which he lives, it also embodies a coming-of-age story. It has the usual components of sexual exploration and the emotional confusion often experienced by teenagers still struggling to understand their hormonal changes. For example, Jamie is infatuated with his best friend, Julie, who frequently spends the night with him, sharing his bed platonically. Julie sneaks out of her house to stay with Jamie, presumably acting out in response to her unhappiness with her mother's remarriage. Her mother—referred to only as "Julie's mother"—is a psychotherapist who forces a rebellious Julie to attend her teen-group counselling sessions. Julie reluctantly agrees to help parent Jamie and does so by watching over him in social situations and giving him lessons on "being a cool guy."

Jamie connects with another stand-in parent, Abbie, a twenty-something-year-old tenant in his mother's boarding house. Abbie is recovering from cervical cancer and worries that she may not be able to bear children. She, therefore, agrees to help Dorothea parent Jamie, albeit, with some reservations and revolutionary strategies not likely to be endorsed by Dorothea. Specifically, she introduces Jamie to punk music, encourages excessive drinking, and gives him lessons in seduction. Jamie appears to connect with Abbie, at one point proclaiming, "I feel like I understand you." Somewhat in sync with Jamie, Abbie emblemizes the late 1970s counterculture attitudes about feminism, music, and culture. Ostensibly out to help Dorothea raise Jamie, Abbie nonetheless enacts a disturbingly subversive interplay between "big sister" and "older, sexually knowledgeable woman" who teaches Jamie about the world of youth rebellion, eroticism, and seduction. Her character intersects with that of both Jamie and Dorothea—at times, she is the mentor and other times, the mentee.

William, the only male tenant in the boarding house, is the final member of this small community. William is a former ex-commune hippy, who meditates and works as a mechanic. Dorothea invites William into their lives, in part, because she wants a male role model for Jamie. William attempts to connect with Jamie, but the fifteen-year-old is generally not receptive to his parental overtures. As the only adult male character in the film, William advances the narrative as a stand-in for the unexplored absence of a biological father in Jamie's life. His presence suggests a significant nod towards traditionalism, which advocates that all children—especially boys—need a father figure to thrive. However, William's overall failure to fill that role adequately casts great doubt on the veracity of this cultural homily.

Through its portrayal of the community of parenting that evolves at Dorothea's pleas, *20th Century Women* invites viewers to contemplate motherhood in more nuanced ways than those promulgated and enforced by traditional Western ideals of parenting. The liberated model of mothering, embedded in the storyline of *20th Century Women*, reimagines parenting as transcending mother's work, which in much public discourse is typically conceptualized as the work of a singular maternal figure. Concurrently, the film transcends the stereotypical dichotomy of good-bad parenting choices by developing characters who comprise a parenting community. The parents in the film—and more specifically, the mothers—are allowed a three dimensionality that is often absent in mainstream media portrayals, thus encouraging a broader position from which to view the often limited binary of understanding good-bad parenting practices.

Reimagining Mothering Through a Parenting Community

Julie: He's my friend. I don't want to be his mom.

Dorothea: Yeah, I know. I'm his mom.

Julie: Don't you need a man to raise a man?

Dorothea: No. I don't think so.

Mediated parenting narratives often centre around one maternal figure—usually, though not always, the biological mother and her parenting choices. *20th Century Women*, in contrast, allows viewers to reimagine this tenet of traditional parenting through its portrayal of a parenting community, which challenges the notion that mothering is synonymous with one maternal figure. Although the film does not discount Dorothea as Jamie's primary caregiver, it supplements her role as a mother with a community of pseudo-parents empowered by the community that does not evolve through traditional social conventions, such as marriage, or organically through unconscious evolution but is instead the conscious creation of Dorothea. *20th Century Women* presents an alternative where women can be active parents who acting in good faith recognize parenting limitations by including and encouraging a range of other community members in the raising of their progeny. Barring the involvement of the community, it is arguable whether what the movie suggests is that individual mothers alone can play these roles played by the different characters and the characters effectively. The reality is that mothering is always facilitated by community involvement whether deliberately or indirectly.

This broadened view of parenting is introduced through the

portrayal of Dorothea's stereotypical struggles with her teenage son. In the beginning moments of the film, viewers are offered several vignettes that juxtapose the mother's and son's attitudes on various topics. For example, the film opens with a depiction of a Ford Galaxy in flames in a grocery store parking lot while Dorothea and Jamie passively watch the burning vehicle from inside the store window. Their different viewpoints on the event are evident:

Dorothea: That was a beautiful car.

Jamie: [scoffs] Mom, it smelled like gas and overheated all the time... and it was just old.

Dorothea: What? Well, it wasn't always old. It just got that way all of a sudden.

The lifecycle of the vehicle is a metaphor for Dorothea's coming to terms with her aging, as her son simultaneously comes of age as a young adult. In another mother-son discussion, at the beginning of the film, Jamie asks his mother a question:

Jamie: Do you think you're happy? Like as happy as you thought you'd be when you were my age?

Dorothea: Seriously? You don't ask people questions like that.

Jamie: You're my mom.

Dorothea: [chuckling] Especially your mom. Look, wondering if you're happy is a great shortcut to just being depressed.

Jamie's nonverbal response shows his frustration and disappointment when his mother uses irony instead of candor to address his earnest question. Dorothea's response might easily be understood by another middle-aged person with similar life experiences, but it is not intelligible to her teenage son. These two interactions, shown in the first fifteen minutes of the film, set up a baseline to view the mother-son relationship as both typical and atypical. Viewers enter the complexity of their relationship at the start of the film, which also creates the justification for constituting a community of pseudo-parents to assist with childrearing. In one sense, each character is constrained by age and positionality; in another, each character transcends their expected stereotypical roles. Jamie demonstrates empathy and compassion for his mother, which indicates an emotional maturity not common in many teenage boys. Dorothea, however, while rebuffing Jamie's attempts to achieve greater intimacy with her, is still more honest than most parents. She offers an explanation to Jamie about her reluctance to grapple with his question.

After establishing the limitations of Dorothea's parenting style, the film transitions to the central plotline in which Dorothea convenes and initiates a community approach to parenting her son. Approximately twenty minutes into the film, Dorothea sits down with Abbie and Julie to request their assistance with Jamie. She explains that her role as a parent has impediments, perhaps in part, due to gender. Consistent with the social-psychological theory, which suggests that boys reject the feminine—specifically, the mother—to become men (Chodorow 110), Dorothea notes: "I have to let go. How do you be a good man? I'm not enough." Dorothea's comments echo Nancy Chodorow's conclusion: "Because they are of different gender than their sons, by contrast, mothers experience their sons as a male opposite.... Sons tend to be experienced as differentiated from their mothers, and mothers push this differentiation (even while retaining, in some cases, a kind of intrusive controlling power over their sons)" (110). Initially, Abbie and Julie are reluctant, but they agree to accept Dorothea's invitation to help parent Jamie. From this point on in the film, viewers are welcomed to interpret parenting through multiple and divergent points of view and through non-traditional parenting practices beginning with Dorothea's involvement of the community in Jamie's rearing. When Julie asks, "Don't you need a man to raise a man?" Dorothea responds with a somewhat qualified, "No. I don't think so." And then she suggests that what is needed instead is a community of people who know and care about her child rather than specific adults occupying socially prescribed roles. In so doing, and as the following pages will argue, the film encourages the audience to associate parenting acts with multiple characters as well as mothering practices by those who are not in primary caregiver roles.

As a result of Dorothea's choices to create a parenting circle for her son, *20th Century Women* builds a transcendent argument of definition, broadening the idea that mothering is synonymous with a single maternal figure. Transcendence helps the rhetor set an issue within a larger context beyond the obvious immediate rhetorical situation. As

Kathryn Olson explains, "Transcendence merges what is inside and outside the boundaries," where "the material on opposite sides of the boundary is not reversed but blended" (133). A transcendence argument does not discount the traditional definition in this case but suggests that parenting may include both the primary caregiver and the community of pseudo-parents. When women, and in particular mothers, seek to enact nontraditional gendered roles, their choices are frequently characterized as problematic. In many cases, they are interpreted as deficient. Suzy D'Enbeau and Patrice Buzzanell observe that "Nonconforming women often are trivialized, stigmatized, and punished for their pursuit of an embodiment of other identities, interests, and lifestyles" (16). In contrast, Dorothea is rewarded for her nonconformist choices as evidenced by a more functional relationship with Jamie, which emerges towards the end of the film. Concluding scenes of the movie show glimpses of a less tension-filled relationship between mother and son, for example in the following exchange:

Jamie: Were you and dad ever in love?

Dorothea: Sure. Or, um... Maybe I was just... I felt I was supposed to be in love. Or I was scared I'd never be in love. So, I just picked the best solution at the time.

In this scene, Dorothea is not sarcastic or dismissive of Jamie's question and responds to him in a better relational way, which has evolved throughout the film. Thus, viewers are encouraged to evaluate and accept her parenting as a success. She is presented as a mother who has developed a more functional interaction with her teenage son because she decided to involve the community of Abbie, Julie, and William in raising him. Instead of asking viewers to privilege either the community or Dorothea, the film provides a vision of parenting that is "both/and" and allows the viewer to identify with options that might appear polarized in a different context. The film, therefore, builds a transcendent foundation to offer a variety of approaches to parenting and, as the next section argues, transgresses dichotomous good-bad mothering categories in the process.

Community Parenting: Transgressing Boundaries of Good and Bad

Abbie: I gave him beer, and then I taught him how to verbally seduce women. And we drove drunk, but I stopped that and then he kissed Trish. And then we walked home.

Dorothea: Ah.

Abbie: You're not mad? You're mad.

According to Heather L. Hayden and Sara E. Hundley, Western culture shares "a definitive understanding of what it means to be a good or bad mom" (2). Moreover, it assesses "maternal practices as starkly good or bad and the 'best' or 'worst' lists offer lessons for real-life moms about how they are expected to behave" (2). *20th Century Women* challenges tenets of traditional mothering through the enactment of mothering tasks by each member of the parenting community, with a range of ambiguous outcomes. Three central tasks regarding motherhood, enacted by different characters throughout the film, emerge as exemplars in both good and bad mothering vignettes: 1) providing advice about transitioning to adulthood; 2) modelling behaviour, and 3) offering comfort. Viewers are invited to understand how mothers may/should enact those behaviours and to reexamine how those enactments are positive or negative examples of mothering. In many respects, these tasks represent the benchmark of assumptions of good mothering in which women assist their offspring in gaining independence while modelling behaviour to inspire the process of maturing and nurturing their children throughout the process. Historically, the central work of good mothering has been to produce young adults who perform their assigned roles in the family as well as in the community, thus contributing to the greater good of all stakeholders. *20th Century Women* does not necessarily challenge that precept but does provide alternative models for how it can be achieved.

Scholars exploring mediated depictions of motherhood have noted how the best mediated mothers are depicted helping children to acclimate to society and transition to adulthood (Dobris and White-Mills, et al.). Good mothers are "selfless and loving" and "remain upbeat and supportive to moody teenagers and grumpy or bumbling spouses.... They offer their maternal insights and love to children who are not their own ... and some are even cool enough to be their kids' best friends" (Hayden and Hundley 1). A significant focus of this coming-of-age story showcases the range of maternal advice offered to Jamie on transitioning to adulthood. Certainly, Dorothea is aware of and articulates the importance of her role in helping Jamie to become what she calls "a good man" and acknowledges her limitations in doing so on her own. But unlike traditional portrayals of mothers in media, Dorothea does not seem to have a clear set of rules, definitions, or a road map for how to get her son to adulthood. Moreover, while she wrestles with some of her choices throughout the film—such as her comfort level with sexual activity, alcohol consumption, and gendered stereotypes—she rarely excoriates herself for not knowing the answers or even for revising the answers she already has taken as given. Dorothea recognizes that a child needs more than the guidance of one parent to achieve a healthy entry into adulthood. However, she also seems to realize that even adults struggle with many of the same issues in a perpetually evolving culture.

In some scenes, Abbie attempts to genuinely play the role of mentor and shares insights with Jamie that ultimately challenge the boundaries of mother-son interactions. For example, she introduces him to feminist scholarship so that he can be a better romantic partner. Dorothea, however, is ambivalent about the usefulness and appropriateness of this information:

> Dorothea: I mean, I appreciate you trying to help. I do. I just think you're taking it too far. This stuff with you know, the women's movement, I respect. But it's just, it's complicated and I think it's too much for him.... He's a fifteen-year-old boy. You're giving him hard core feminism and it...
>
> Abbie: But he really loves it, and it's really, it's helping him...
>
> Dorothea: Helping him what?
>
> Abbie: It's helping him become a man. What you were talking about.
>
> Dorothea: Learning about a female orgasm is helping him be a man?
>
> Abbie: Well, what man do you know that cares anything about that? I mean, that's a miracle.

In this exchange, Dorothea challenges Abbie's introduction of Jamie to some feminist ideas. Certainly, the concept of new manhood concerned with female orgasm in a heterosexual relationship is at odds with most traditional concepts of masculinity for a maturing male. In this scene, Dorothea seems constrained by traditional expectations—even possibly, by modesty—which is a departure from her earlier position and actions in the film, when she is portrayed more progressively. Viewers are offered two mindsets in the same situation: one presumably progressive (Abbie) and the other traditional (Dorothea). By juxtaposing the perspectives of the two characters, viewers are encouraged to identify with Abbie and Dorothea, and, as such, are invited to evaluate Abbie's parenting strategies on their terms.

Seventeen-year-old Julie's parenting approach concentrates on Jamie's physical wellbeing. Like Abbie's approach, Julie's method includes instructions on how to attract women. Julie makes a sincere attempt to offer maternal advice to Jamie, explaining: "I think being strong is the most important quality. It's not being vulnerable; it's not being sensitive. It's not even ... honestly, it's not even being happy. It's about strength and your durability against the other emotions." Here, Julie is portrayed as having a potentially positive influence on Jamie, when contrasted with some of her encouraging Jamie to smoke. Scholars interrogating representations of good and bad mothers in popular discourse have typically concluded that mothers are rewarded for good behaviour and punished for bad behaviour (Davidson and Stache; D'Enbeau and Buzzanell; Lehman). Viewers observe aspects of so-called good, and bad mothering, and in-between mothering behaviors to discourage them from assigning fixed and dichotomous valuations of Julie as either a good or bad mother. By "deviating from the good/bad binary" *20th Century Women* offers "more nuanced portraits of mothers and mothering" (Hayden and Hundley 2). Julie is shown as a complex young woman; she is flawed but her parenting role has a positive role in this setting.

The storyline complicates these moments of presumably good mothering advice with examples of more questionable instruction. For example, Abbie walks into Jamie's room after a night of drinking and catches Jamie and Julie sharing a bed. She tells Jamie: "You cannot let her sleep here if she's not having sex with you. It's disempowering." In this instance, Abbie seems compelled to give what she sees as parental advice to Jamie. Viewers are presented with a multifaceted scene that seems inappropriate. Yet viewers are also invited to see Abbie's advice as an important relationship lesson. In a traditional context, a parent might be expected to condemn the cosleeping of teenagers of different sexes rather than recommend the sexualization of such an asexual relationship. Abbie's age and outsider's position in Jamie's life make her advice unusual. However, viewers recall that it is Jamie's mother who facilitated this relationship. Dorothea could be held responsible for any perceived parenting lapses, including ignorance of her son's sharing of his bed with Julie when she sleeps over. She encourages Julie, who in some ways is an unstable young woman, to play the role of an advisor to Jamie. Dorothea is unable to teach Jamie; so Julie, acting the role of peer pressure, teaches him. Julie teaches Jamie about temptation from a woman. Abbie's statement then complements Julie's actions. Thus, Julie's advice resonates with Dorothea's intentions. In heterosexual relations, males and females are not typically allowed cosleeping privileges outside of sexual liaisons. What might be dismissed in some contexts as bad parenting provokes reflection on taken-for-granted assumptions about romantic relationships and parental advice on such relations.

The complexity of good or bad parenting advice is further illustrated in a scene where Abbie and William offer advice to Jamie at Dorothea's dinner party. After Dorothea instructs Jamie to "please wake up Abbie" when she appears to be asleep at the table, Abbie responds:

Abbie: I'm menstruating.

Dorothea: Abbie, you know what? Ok. You're menstruating, but do you have to say it? Okay. Do we really need to know everything that's going on with you?

Abbie: What? I'm menstruating. Why is that a big deal?

Dorothea: We don't need to hear about that. Thank you.

Abbie: [Directed toward Jamie but the entire table hears] If you ever want to have an adult relationship with a woman, like if you want to have sex with a woman's vagina, you need to be comfortable with the fact that the vagina menstruates and just say menstruation. It's not a big deal.

William then advises Jamie: "Sex during menstruation can be very pleasurable for a woman. It can even, like, relieve some of the cramps. Jamie, I also wanna say never have sex with just the vagina. You have to have sex with the whole woman." For many, Abbie's introduction of menstruation and William's interjection on sexual intercourse as topics at a dinner that includes a teenage boy and his mother, as well as other guests, will at least appear uncomfortable if not wildly inappropriate. But the film does not shy away from uncomfortable scenes and allows the conversation to play out without establishing a clear evaluation of either side. Is Abbie progressive or merely inappropriate because she broaches a taboo topic in an incongruous setting? Is Dorothea repressed or perspicacious because she tries to steer the conversation away from the topic, ultimately attempting to nix its discussion? Although arguably inappropriate as dinner table banter, Abbie and William's interjections are offered as good intentioned, meant to give Jamie insight into women, albeit sexually.

In scenes that centre on advice giving, examples of maternal advice that might foster Jamie's development into adulthood are presented for reflection. In some senses, the film reinforces patriarchal assumptions about sexuality that suggest that becoming a man is primarily about heterosexual sex. Instead of encouraging views about the characters as either good or bad based on parental advice on sexuality, viewers are called to reconceptualize and reflect on more complex parenting practices. There is a certain logic to much of the advice, however unusual the packaging; viewers can choose to evaluate both traditional and nontraditional advice and draw their own conclusions. For example, Julie explains to the virginal, teenage Jamie that she cannot describe female orgasms because she "doesn't have them" and "none of my friends do." When he is confused about why she or any woman would desire sexual intimacy without the promise of orgasm, she explains: "There's other reasons. You know, like the way that he looks at you. Or the way they get a little bit desperate at some point. And the little sounds that they make. And their bodies ... cause you don't exactly know what they're gonna look like, or smell or feel like until you do it. But, yeah, half the time I regret it." Jamie has the unique opportunity to understand heterosexual sex from at least one feminine vantage point, and the audience can choose to see this interaction as either inappropriate or progressive, depending on their viewpoint. In another scene, after a night of underage drinking, an inebriated Abbie offers this advice to Jamie about his relationship with Julie: "You can't let her push you around. You have to tell her what you want." In this interaction, viewers might side with Abbie, agreeing that Julie seems to tease Jamie sexually without following through. But given Jamie's youthful ignorance about sex, the advice may seem inappropriate at this time if not confusing to Jamie.

Stephanie L. Gomez indicates that in contemporary Western culture, mothers "are supposed to be rational, dignified, mature, and in control of themselves" (150). Dorothea's behaviours in certain ways challenge these idealized images of the mother. By constantly smoking around her son, Dorothea appears to exhibit signs of bad parenting, even by 1970s standards, and this undermines the model of the mother as an ideal human. Similarly, this model posits that no good mother should abdicate her role to surrogate parents who exhibit non-normative behaviours. As noted earlier, Abbie parents Jamie, in part, by taking him to bars, buying him a beer, and teaching him how to seduce women. Instead of responding critically, Dorothea tells Abbie: "You get to see him out in the world as a person. I never will." Her response accomplishes two aims. First, the limits of traditional mothering are exposed. Second, the implied negative aspects of parenting (e.g., Abbie's negligent choices) and imputed positive choices (e.g., Dorothea's ability to see the good in this lesson) are both thrown into sharp relief for reevaluation. The dualistic portrayal of parenting behaviours creates a nuanced representation of parenting crafted to avoid binary labelling of maternal figures. Traditional notions of mothering are not embraced, nor is a false dichotomy established between parenting by the mother and parenting by the community. The range of acceptable choices offered, suggests that it is possible to fail at some aspects of parenting while succeeding at others.

Jamie's community of parental figures frequently models "self-serving and sexual" behaviour, which Hayden and Hundley indicate are descriptors of the "worst moms" in media portrayals (1). As argued by Rachel D. Davidson, Catherine A. Dobris, and Kim White-Mills, the definition of "bad mothering" can appear synonymous with stereotypes of irresponsible male behaviour (2). For example, Julie practices risky sexual encounters with multiple young men, which she describes in graphic detail to Jamie. Intended as an indirect message to

Jamie that she is available to try out with him, her stories nonetheless make Jamie jealous while perhaps also turning him off. Besides, Julie's regime of regularly sleeping in Jamie's bed may be interpreted as sexual domination. Although Julie eschews any sexual relationship with him, she still tempts him in the following ways: She would ask him to stroke her arm while regurgitating the philosophies on sex expounded by pulp fiction writer Judy Blume and pop psychologist Scott Peck. Although Julie's behaviour in no way conforms to ideas on healthy, interpersonal relationships, especially among teen peers, it reveals Julie's neediness in contrast to Jamie's apparent infatuation with her. Certainly, their asexual interactions pose difficulties for Jamie, as he facilitates Julie's self-seeking indulgence. The question raised here is what are the lessons Jamie learns from his relationship with his interaction with Julie and how they might influence his development into a healthy sexual and emotional being. Dorothea, Abbie, and Julie seem to fail at enacting the ideal traditional roles of good mothering, even if the complexity of scenes allows for a consideration of potentially positive outcomes for Jamie.

In other respects, when Julie at times is not overstepping male-female boundaries in her physical relationship with Jamie, she demonstrates a caring behaviour. For example, when Jamie blacks out at a skate park in front of a group of young friends, Julie is the only person who runs to his aid. She is panic stricken when he does not respond to her frantic shaking of him, and she screams at others to go for help. In this scene, Julie steps up to perform the role of a concerned and empathetic friend who will ensure a friend's safety. The juxtaposition of Julie's conflicting behaviours blurs any distinctions between concepts of good or bad mothering. Through the continuous balancing of good and bad mothering behaviours, made by both Dorothea and the community of pseudo-parents, *20th Century Women* transgresses the problematic good-bad dichotomy.

In contemporary Western culture, mothers are expected to be nurturing, and as indicated by Stephanie L. Gomez, mothers "who nurture and sacrifice for their children may be perceived as far better than mothers who exhibit less outwardly affectionate qualities" (152). Throughout most of the film, Dorothea frequently does not provide comfort to Jamie in situations where such support might be expected. For example, the film portrays scenes in which Jamie attempts to better understand his mother. In one such scene, Jamie reads Zoe Moss's essay "It Hurts to Be Alive and Obsolete" aloud to his mother. The essay is a reflection on what it means to be a middle-aged woman to solicit empathy for middle-aged women and initiate dialogue. Instead of appreciating her son's efforts, Dorothea appears offended by this and summarily dismisses him: "You think you know me better because you read that? Why are you reading it to me?" On the one hand, this scene calls on younger viewers to sympathize with Jamie while representing Dorothea as a cavalier, disgruntled, and disinterested mother. On the other hand, older viewers may connect with Dorothea's discomfort in response to her son's broaching of topics that are intensely personal for her, which the young Jamie cannot possibly yet comprehend. In another instance, Dorothea demonstrates a lack of nurturance when she responds with sarcasm after observing Julie and Jamie saying goodbye to each other at a party. Dorothea smirks at their show of affection, prompting the following exchange:

Jamie: Stop.

Dorothea: What.

Jamie: Thinking that you know everything that's going on.

Dorothea: No, I don't. I just think that, you know, having your heart broken is a tremendous way to learn about the world. [Dorothea smiles and walks away from Jamie.]

As Jamie's mother and primary caregiver, Dorothea is expected to enact a more sympathetic mothering role after witnessing a tender interaction between Jamie and his closest female friend. Instead, *20th Century Women* presents a transgressive mother who is somewhat insensitive to her child's feelings. Alternatively, she could also be feeling a bit jealous of the attention Julie seems to be getting from Jamie, which Dorothea craves for. There is a latent fear of losing Jamie to Julie. These all paint a picture of a flawed and imperfect mother—a mother who invites a complex character and mothering performance evaluation. Dorothea's character helps the film advance an invitational argument on the benefits of a community approach to parenting. Through her combination of traditional and nontraditional parenting practices, Dorothea advocates a challenge to an earlier claim that "she is not enough" and that her parenting practices involving a community comprising Abbie, Julie, and William, with questionable backgrounds and histories of irresponsible behaviours, are all necessarily bad for Jamie. By simultaneously presenting viewers with good and bad parenting examples, the film attempts to "offer a perspective" without "seeking its acceptance" (Foss and Griffin 7). As argued in the next section, by reimagining mothering through community and transgressing boundaries of good-bad dichotomies, *20th Century Women* reveals a liberated model of mothering.

A Liberated Model of Mothering through Transcendence

20th Century Women provides a complex depiction of motherhood by illustrating the intersections of community, friendship, and parenting. As such, it offers a position on childrearing that broadens the cultural ideals of Western motherhood. It helps to produce and project workable counternarratives to traditional patriarchal principles of mothering. The film tables for reflection a wider and liberated understanding of mothering through the inclusion of community and friends in the parenting process. This liberated model of mothering as presented in *20th Century Women* destabilizes the good-bad depiction of mothering. The film's collective vision of childrearing is consistent with Foss and Griffin's model that proffers a celebratory vision of parenting that includes and embraces imperfect and contradictory "unique and individual identities" (11). The liberated model of mothering is reinforced in the conclusion of the movie through its creation of a complex process of identification between viewers and characters. Film studies critic Murray Smith argues that identification or "engagement" (35) is fostered when viewers develop "spatial attachment" and are provided "subjective access" to characters (41). Spatial attachment is defined by Smith as occurring when the spectator is asked to follow the narrative of a character, whereas subjective access refers to the "degree of access we have to the subjectivity of characters" (41).

20th Century Women encourages viewers to complete the process of spatial attachment. Viewers are also given subjective access to characters through flashforwards. Dorothea reveals that she is diagnosed with cancer in 1999. Then, Julie says she leaves her hometown to attend NYU, losing touch with Dorothea, Jamie, and her mother. She tells viewers that she falls in love, moves to Paris, and decides not to have children. Abbie, however, details that she stays in Santa Barbara, falls in love, works as an artist, and has two boys. Next, William reveals that he opens a pottery store, marries, and then later gets divorced. Finally, Jamie finishes Dorothea's story and connects it with his own. He explains that Dorothea meets a man named Jim, and they are happily married until she dies of cancer two decades later. After Dorothea's death, Jamie is married and has a son. He promises that he will try to explain to his child who and what his grandmother was like. But the implication that this "will be impossible" undermines the movie's intention to reconstruct a comprehensive historical account of the complicated relationship between Jamie and his mother. The movie provides only a glimpse into this complicated history, but each of the characters appears to find some measure of happiness and peace in the future. By narrating outcomes to their individual stories, the characters demonstrate agency and autonomy and invite viewers to consider the implications of choices made earlier in the film. A closure is provided for each character, suggesting to viewers that everyone turns out okay and that the atypical approach to parenting created a positive outcome for Jamie. By circumventing the good-bad binary of mothering, typical in most media portrayals of motherhood, *20th Century Women* presents a compelling argument for privileging the influence of a complex community in the childrearing process.

Conclusions and Implications for Future Research

20th Century Women is an invitation to understand motherhood as a complex series of mothering practices often involving collective parenting. Within the collective efforts of friends, family, and community, there evolves a framework which—if we are to believe the facile wrap up of the film—ultimately functions, with all its imperfections, to educate an adolescent boy through to adulthood. *20th Century Women* also invites the contemplation of alternative perspectives on motherhood, challenging traditional tenets of patriarchal defined motherhood. Through contemplation of collective parenting as an alternative to the traditional nuclear family, nontraditional parenting options may be validated, whereas tenets of traditional parenting may also prove practicable.

Foss and Griffin suggest that invitational rhetoric creates an environment where "the ideas that can be considered multiply" (16). In contrast to Aristotelian rhetorical practice, "rather than the discovery of how to make a case, invitational rhetoric employs invention to discover more cases" (16). As an embodiment of invitational rhetoric, *20th Century Women* functions to stimulate questions and allows for "diverse positions to be compared in a process of discovery and questioning that may lead to transformation for themselves and others" (6). The audience is not dispatched a new and improved replacement for the nuclear family, since many of the inadequacies of Dorothea's alternatives are highlighted throughout the film. Instead, we are provided a basis from which to question traditional assumptions. Do boys need fathers or father figures to grow up well? Can nonparents help to raise good children? What roles should parents play in helping their progeny come of age? Questions are posed subliminally through the narrative but are not answered except in the minds of the audience.

Our analysis of *20th Century Women* speaks to mothering identity at a particular place in time, on the cusp of the twenty-first century, when women's identity as tied to motherhood is being challenged by a myriad of other factors, such as employment, equality in gender roles, and increasing childcare options. The plotline of this film is ostensibly about the rearing of Jamie, yet the title itself suggests a different emphasis on the part of the rhetors. Perhaps the film's title implies that we cannot discuss mothers' identities without also discussing implications for their children. Or perhaps, Jamie's coming-of-age story is only a vehicle for examining women's changing roles in this pivotal, historical period. Regardless, the film urges contemplation and discourse about women's identities in the twenty-first century as it relates to the sociocultural identities that comprise those communities.

Foss and Griffin observe that "The inclusion of an invitational rhetoric in the array of rhetoric available avers the need to revise and expand rhetorical constructs of various kinds to take into account the nature and function of this form" (16). Through the application of an invitational rhetorical frame to *20th Century Women*, liberated viewpoints on motherhood in public discourse are revealed and, consistent with this theoretical framework, offer "a mode of communication for women and other marginalized groups to use in their efforts to transform systems of domination and oppression" (16). As such, *20th Century*

Women reveals how rhetors might "disengage from the dominance and mastery so common to a system of oppression and create a reality of equality and mutuality in its place, allowing for options and possibilities not available within the familiar, dominant framework" (17). From this perspective, we see complex and flawed characters who demonstrate enigmatic behaviours, thus inviting viewers to examine diverse mothering practices. And as with all invitations, viewers may accept or reject in every instance, as they make sense of the range of options offered in the construction of motherhood. *20th Century Women* contributes to a contemporary, popular media landscape in ways that do not provide answers to questions but rather provoke scrupulous discussion on motherhood and community.

Works Cited

20th Century Women. Directed by Mike Mills, performances by Annette Bening, Elle Fanning, Greta Gerwig, Billy Crudup, and Lucas Jade Zumann, A24, 2016.

Boser, Beth. "'I Forgot How It Was to Be Normal': Decompensating the Binary of Good/Bad Mothering." *Mediated Moms: Contemporary Challenges to the Motherhood Myth*, edited by Heather. L. Hundley and Sara E. Hayden, Peter Lang Publishing, 2016, pp. 161-81.

Chodorow, Nancy. *The Reproduction of Mothering: Psychoanalysis and the Sociology of Gender.* Yale University Press, 1978.

Davidson, Rachel D. "Disrupting and Containing Motherhood: Challenging Subversive Representations in *Waitress* and *Frozen River*." *Screening Mothers: Motherhood in Contemporary World Cinemas*, edited by Asma Sayed, Demeter Press, 2016, pp. 132-49.

Davidson, Rachel D., Catherine A. Dobris, and Kim White-Mills. "What Makes a "Bad" Mom "Bad"?: A Critical Review of Lucas and Moore's *Bad Moms*." *Women and Language*, vol. 41, no. 2, pp. 171-73.

Davidson, Rachel D., and Lara C. Stache. "A Tale of Morality, Class, and Transnational Mothering: Broadening and Constraining Motherhood in *Mammoth*." *Mediated Moms: Contemporary Challenges to the Motherhood Myth*, edited by Heather. L. Hundley and Sara E. Hayden, Peter Lang Publishing, 2016, pp. 183-202.

D'Enbeau, Suzy, and Patrice M. Buzzanell. "Counter-Intensive Mothering: Exploring Transgressive Portrayals and Transcendence on Mad Men." *Mediated Moms: Contemporary Challenges to the Motherhood Myth*, edited by Heather. L. Hundley and Sara E. Hayden, Peter Lang Publishing, 2016, pp. 183-202.

Dobris, Catherine A., et al. "The *Spockian Mother*: Images of the 'Good' Mother in Dr. Spock's *The Common Sense Book of Baby and Child Care*, 1946-1992." *Communication Quarterly*, vol. 65, no. 1, 2016, pp. 39-59.

Foss, Sonja. K., and Cindy L. Griffin. "Beyond Persuasion: A Proposal for an Invitational Rhetoric." *Communication Monographs*, vol. 62, 1995, pp. 2-18.

Gomez, Stephanie L. "'Save Your Tears for Your Pillow: Tough Love and the Mothering Double Bind in Dance Moms." *Mediated Moms: Contemporary Challenges to the Motherhood Myth. Mediated Moms: Contemporary Challenges to the Motherhood Myth*, edited by Heather. L. Hundley and Sara E. Hayden, Peter Lang Publishing, 2016, pp. 143-60.

Hayden, Heather L., and Sara E. Hundley. "Introduction: Challenging the Motherhood Myth." *Mediated Moms: Contemporary Challenges to the Motherhood Myth*, edited by Heather. L. Hundley and Sara E. Hayden, Peter Lang Publishing, 2016, pp. 1-13.

Lehman, Katherine J. "Addicted to Danger: The Fierce, Flawed Mothers of Nurse Jackie and Weeds." *Mediated Moms: Contemporary Challenges to the Motherhood Myth*, edited by Heather. L. Hundley and Sara E. Hayden, Peter Lang Publishing, 2016, pp. 53-76.

Olson, Kathryn, M. "The Controversy over President Reagan's Visit to Bitburg: Strategies of Definition and Redefinition." *Quarterly Journal of Speech*, vol. 75, no. 2, 1989, pp. 129-51.

O'Reilly, Andrea. *Mother Outlaws: Theories and Practices of Empowered Mothering*. Women's Press, 2004.

Podnieks, Elizabeth. "'I Really Need a Mom Right Now': Maternal Absence, Ambivalence, and Autonomy in *Glee*." *The Journal of Popular Culture*, vol. 49, no. 4, 2016, pp. 897-916.

Rich, Adrienne. *Of Woman Born: Motherhood as Experience and Institution*. W. W. Norton and Company, 1986.

Smith, Murry. "Altered States: Character and Emotional Response in the Cinema." *Cinema Journal*, vol. 33, no. 4, 1994, pp. 34-56.

Chapter 6

Mma Habiba: Maternal Outcast or Community Mother

Dannabang Kuwabong

I wish I could recount my puerile memories
Memories of furtive voices of her children
Memories still like repeating echoes
From dreaded Moritanga, the arrowhead of hills
Where Mma Habiba camped her maternal mystery
Above the cave where twin-headed pythons
Whispered stories about her children that walked
Who had swooped down on Sarankyi Mori's Sofas (Wilks 123-24)
Swept them like dry leaves across the Black Volta[1]
Who had risen to defend her children in Nanvilli
And squelched Babatu and his Zabarima slavers (Tuurey 56-62)

I wish I could recount our puerile memories
Memories of furtive voices of her children
Memories, still, like repeating echoes
To recall why she became a hermit in our midst
A lone shadow of our desire to neglect
The womb that nourished our spirits
Some called her Habiba Ma, others Mma Habiba
Why we never asked or cared to ponder

Beyond shallow songs to dance on her shadow
Prancing like amazing newborn calves
Singing like frightened weaver birds:

> *Habiba ma*   *Habiba's mother*
> *Sing-kaa pɛbɛ*   *immature peanuts*
> *Ɔɔra yaara*   *chewing spilling*

Her presence excited all, adults and kids
Children who sucked thumps or sniffed smut
Gazed with wide pupils and quivering lips
As she threaded softly through village paths
Casting blessings in her greetings to all
Walking past the shadow of her prime
No one seemed to remember her real name
Except that she was Habiba Ma/Mma Habiba
A Faling-Tang Zupili Ma, a Nanvilli Kuuroo Ma[2]
None could claim eternal motherhood like her
Yet we the children never failed to sing and dance

> *Habiba ma*   *Habiba's mother*
> *Sing-kaa pɛbɛ*   *immature peanuts*
> *Ɔɔra yaara*   *chewing spilling*

No other mother figure could walk like her
Could imitate the beauty of her smile or walk
Her hair, a lush grove that shaded her face
Must have startled savannah covered heads
Her calves and hunches encircled by beads
Waistline and backline articulate in language
Eyes that glittered with love for all woman born
A voice that trembled with care for all little ones
Her arms strong yet radiating supple gentleness
And yet she walked in the silence of her mystery
And yet we the kids pranced and sang our song

MMA HABIBA: MATERNAL OUTCAST OR COMMUNITY MOTHER

>   *Habiba ma*   *Habiba's mother*
>   *Sing-kaa pɛbɛ*   *immature peanuts*
>   *Ɔɔra yaara*   *chewing spilling*

Her gliding silhouette rose against the rising sunrays
Balanced a pot of water from Kuuroo
Her striding silhouette defied the sinking sunrays
Smoke from her hermitage filtering through
Every aperture in the homes of families
We wondered what she cooked and what she ate
For no one ever saw her buy food from the market
And no one ever caught her stealing from their farms
And yet she exuded a beauty of joy unknown to us
We the children and other mothers only imagined
Why she lived alone on Nanvilli's dread Hill. Alone.

>   *Habiba ma*   *Habiba's mother*
>   *Sing-kaa pɛbɛ*   *immature peanuts*
>   *Ɔɔra yaara*   *chewing spilling*

She picked herbs with the first rains
Beside other women with crying babies
She helped wives and mothers sow peanuts
In the season of sowing crops in distant farms
She was there to gather shea nuts in the bushes
She was there to decorate new homes of others
And never whispered a complaint against any
And all called her Habiba Ma or Mma Habiba
Though there was no Habiba in Nanvilli
She worked besides women whose children sang
She worked beside men whose children danced

>   *Habiba ma*   *Habiba's mother*
>   *Sing-kaa pɛbɛ*   *immature peanuts*
>   *Ɔɔra yaara*   *chewing spilling*

We the children would wander in intrigue
Asking the wind to whisper to us the secret
Mma Habiba where is she from? Without friends?
The wind only caressed its lips and blew away
Was her daughter named Habiba then?
Did she lose her to a comother with an evil eye?
Did she lose her husband's attention then?
Why did she sing lullabies along the village paths?
Bringing smiles to other mothers frowning faces
When dusk heard mother's anxious voices calling kids
Among the scattered and crowded homesteads?
Impatient to wait we sang and danced

> *Habiba ma*   *Habiba's mother*
> *Sing-kaa pɛbɛ*   *immature peanuts*
> *Ɔɔra yaara*   *chewing spilling*

Today, stranded, confused unable to sing
I shiver and hum without tune or dance
At the crossing of Calle Salamanca and Calle Duke
That Maria and Irma sisters could tear away
Children from teats of laughter and hope
Lick and kick children in the groins and chins
Make us recall the agony of tears and despair
I wish I could recount my puerile memories
Memories of furtive voices of her children
Memories, still, like repeating echoes
I wish I could recount my puerile memories
Memories of furtive voices of children
Memories, still, like repeating echoes
I would gather my tattered courage
Walk back to you in supplication
Drink deep the mysteries of your eyes
Soak in the assurance of your smiles
And call you Mma. And call you Mma.
Mma mine ma. My mother's mother

She who prevailed against evil in life
Sing and dance with a new song and rhythm:

Habiba ma	*Habiba's mother*
Sing-kaa pɛbɛ	*immature peanuts*
Ɔɔra yaara	*chewing spilling*

I wish I could recount my puerile memories
Memories of furtive voices of children
Memories, still, like repeating echoes
Alas. Too late for the fractured memory
Can no longer mend what is broken
But I see you in all mothers now.
Mma Habiba, Habiba Ma. Rest in my heart.

Endnotes

1. A river that starts in Mali and runs through Burkina Faso, runs along the northwestern border of Ghana, divides Ghana and Côte d'Ivoire, and finally merges with the White Volta to form the Volta Lake in Ghana.
2. Names assigned to daughters of the Ekoala Clan (Leopard Clan) of Nanvilli. Faling-Tang is an area covered by mushroom termite hills. Kuuroo is a spring whose water enabled the first settlers to thrive.

Works Cited

Tuurey, G. *An Introduction to the Mole-Speaking Community*. Wa Catholic Press, 1982.

Wilkes, Ivor. *Wa and the Wala Islam and polity in northwestern Ghana*. Cambridge University Press, 1989.

Chapter 7

Maria's Maternal Rage against the Community

Dannabang Kuwabong

I

you awaken on the day of Maria's rage
meet your nightmares strolling
on these Islas del encantes,
these ravaged Comunidades
where Los tourists seek escape
dreams of abundant ecstasies
but today you cringe startled
locked inside your hotel toilet
afraid of the roars of competing winds
of the wrath of boiling seas
no one to transfer your fear of hurricanes

the leaves of Eden are sheered
strewn, raked, and gathered
the land dry-eyed lies lacerated
new gullies chopped by sharp waters
and mud armies ride boulders
down these ancient valleys
join your granite of nightmare

you bite your quivering lips
your fingers bloodied on rosary beads
as you chant litanies of saints
you recall a hymn long despised
after your confirmation on the Feast of Assumption:

Hail, Queen of heav'n, the ocean star!
Guide of the wand'rer here below!
Thrown on life's surge, we claim thy care;
save us from peril and from woe.
Mother of Christ, star of the sea,
pray for the wanderer, pray for me

sucked in by airwave promises
you await the count of losses
for words, for feeling, for faith
confirmed in your surrounding:
and you belong no more.

you recall only how that night
how Maria's panyaring acts
on these Islas del encantes
began a new way of calling time

you recall the whooping winds
batter in roofs, splinter hurricane shutters
you can revision the bulbous waters
rise to challenge concrete walls
Fabaceae crash in supplication dance
their prayers bring no pardons

this then is what the ancients foresaw
that nature's ritual dances of death
take back in swift flashes of power
what you worship as normal
think you control, modify, own
now you stand dismayed
in this place of sublime pleasure
a soul's shadow in coming days
a little taste of fear in your sojourn:

Sojourners in this vale of tears,
To thee, blest advocate, we cry.
Oh, pity our sorrows, calm our fears.
And soothe with hope our misery.
Refuge in grief, Star of the sea,
Pray for the mourner, Oh, pray for me.

you wonder whether your sins
brought Maria's vengeance
on these sinless virgin islands.

II

After the Passover of Irma and Maria
On these Virgin and enchanted islands
We who, spared of the slashes of death
By wind and flying aluminum sheets
Or pounded, pummelled, scattered
By falling trees or flung bricks from rooftops
We stand at street corners
Seeing nothing, recognizing nothing
Eyeing evidence of our nakedness
No promises of safety on land or sea
No promises of safety from sky or soil
Only the brazen sun smiles at its rising to its setting
Only the winking stars, twinkle in the darkness
Only the steam of the still air hangs like a wet overcoat
We question our existence on these rocks in the sea
we lift our drooping heads, wandering in a daze
mouths open with no breath to exhale our pain
We turn and we turn, trudging into ruined castles
We spin and we spin, stooping under blankets of heat
Wondering: is this how the children of Pharaoh felt
When the angel of vengeance stopped at their doors
Because they were unmarked by a lamb's blood?
For Maria and Irma must be lieutenants
Of that angel that spilled innocent blood.

Chapter 8

Fifty-Five Miles

Heather Robinson

She's ferocious, the nurse says,
As Caroline latches so hard she makes blisters.
After all the blood and worry,
I am thrilled that my little girl can eat.
And eat she did, all the time—
I called her a succubus as I nursed her
Most of the minutes of most of the hours.

I didn't know before she was born,
How much I would need someone to talk to
About breasts and milk and latches and tongues.
How much I would need to listen
To talk that made me normal,
That reassured me that things would change.

We would go to La Leche League.
La-shay-shay, the little girl called it.
I was scandalized by this eighteen-month-old
Sipping from her mother's breast,
Playing then sipping,
Looking around and grinning,
Then sipping.
Her mother just held her breast right there
Ready.
I had not yet been bellowed at by my own
Uh side booby!
I had not yet been entreated on repeat

KiKi?
But I sat on the floor and listened and it all slowly
Made more sense.

In those days I was just a mum
Three short and long months.
Three months in one place.
I was learning how to stay still.
Just be.
Leave meant I could leave
Stay off the train, stay out of the city,
Try to find my people where I live.

We spent our time visiting white women in subdivisions,
Solving the puzzle that was the baby.
We would cross the broad lawn of the leader's house,
The landscaper's signs next to those of the local Republican congressman.
The leaders were quite excited—
You know, we have another two-mom family
We love having two-mom families
You are welcome here.

Back at home, Caroline sleeps on my lap
Twenty minutes out of every two hours.
I perch my laptop on the nursing pillow
Writing a book that may never be finished.
I answer the door and make coffee.
My friend tells me about her friends—
Jen, Carly, Sarah, Amanda—
Mothers, all of us,
As though they are in my world
As though I am in theirs.
I just nod and say ah.

White woman academic seeks someone
Anyone
Who can talk mothering and academia at the same time?

FIFTY-FIVE MILES

White woman academic,
Long-term breastfeeder,
Seeks friend to talk about Big Things with.
White woman academic,
Plays stay-at-home mom
But isn't one.

My audience, these women
sitting in suburban great rooms,
drinking coffee on my sofa,
My mothering friends
From La Leche League,
From the bakery,
From story time at the library,
They don't see that my performance
Is held up by a full-time job
Fifty-five miles away from home.

Leave over, I travel alone, family tucked away.
Three trains, commuter rail.
Newark, Manhattan, Jamaica.
Queens. At the end of the ride,
Mothers, children, strollers again. Moving.
I walk alongside them
On my way to work.

II.
Motherhood and Friendship

Chapter 9

Supportive and Destructive Female Relationships in Mariama Bâ's *So Long a Letter*

Sherean Shehada

> I have received your letter. By way of reply, I am beginning this diary, my prop in my distress. Our long association has taught me that confiding in others allays pain. (Bâ 1)

> Friendship has splendor that love knows not. It grows stronger when crossed, whereas obstacles kill love. Friendship resists time, which wearies and severs couples. It has heights unknown to love. (Bâ 156)

In the epithet above, the protagonist in *So Long a Letter*, Ramatoulaye (Rama), clearly states her dilemma. The second sets the tone of *So Long A Letter*: the use of faith and friendship as tools for managing grief and hardships in relationships, love, and life. The letter is addressed to her friend Aissatou, who now lives in France. She had divorced her husband for his betrayal of their romantic marriage agreement and the hostility of his mother and family towards her. In their collective sisterly suffering, Rama writes the following words, which set the focus of this chapter: "We were true sisters, destined for the same mission of emancipation" (16). Rama has faith and hope in this friendship, this nurturing friendship, and the community of the victimized that provides the space for empowerment. Solomon Omatsola Azumurana's argument that "the promise and problem of an economically empowered African woman are, at a level, the subject of the novel" (qtd. in Azumurana 8) underscores the philosophy of my argument. I explore the personal and social complications and struggles of Ramatoulaye, a Western-educated and middle-class woman, who marries for love, despite her mother's reservations, and whose husband, after twenty-five years and twelve children, decides to take a teenager as a wife. Moreover, I examine how Ramatoulaye achieves a balance between her religious demands and her roles as a wife and mother in patriarchal Senegalese society. Despite the constrictions of patriarchal domination, Ramatoulaye can negotiate between the desires of the self and the roles of the adult female in which she refuses to abandon because she has been, "reared since childhood on their strict precepts" (Bâ 9).

So Long A Letter is not just a mere exchange of gossip between two dear and childhood friends. The novel is about a strong friendship that helps both Rama and Aissatou to support each other to alleviate their pain. I argue that it is the power and reliability of these female-centred and motherhood-centred friendships that sustain Ramatoulaye in her ordeal of betrayal. This friendship between mothers is what lifts Rama during the forty days of mourning Modou, as designated by Islam. The depth of their friendship is the well from which they each draw strength. Thus, friendship among women is highly valued in Senegalese society—be they mothers in monogamous or polygamous marriages, Western educated or not. Bâ plays with the idea of a woman who engages a multipronged approach to find harmony in the complicated aspects of her life: Ramatoulaye the mother of twelve children; Ramatoulaye the deserted wife and mother; and Ramatoulaye the widow, whose recent status adds extra challenges to her already constricted existence as a female. Thus, the novel asks important questions. How does one restore faith in human relationships? How can a mother still survive without suffering a psychoemotional breakdown as in the case of Jacqueline or experiencing anger and rebellion as demonstrated by her friend Aissatou? In this chapter, I explore the representation of sisterhood in the narrative beyond the representation of wifehood and widowhood. Sisterhood is a rich fountain of support and care—a source that provides both solace and solidarity among women during traumatic events such as divorce, death, and betrayal in polygamous societies. Sisterhood as a woman-to-woman bond prepares Rama to "survive socially, economically, and above all emotionally after Modou, her husband" (d'Almeida 161). Because of sisterhood, Rama becomes a self-reliant and self-assured middle-aged woman as well as a fountain of love and support to her family and friend Aissatou. The second part of this chapter explores how sometimes women's empowerment can be undermined by other women whose selfishness prevents them from seeing the wider picture of helping other women to reclaim their voice and agency. For example, Aunt Nabou and Lady Mother-in-Law obstruct women's efforts to raise women above their oppression and humiliation.

Sisterhood, or in Clenora Hudson-Weems words "community of women" (*Africana Womanism* 65), gives Rama the tools she needs to rediscover her worth as an Africana woman with a mind, body, and soul and who can squeeze success out of desperate situations. Thus, Rama transcends "victimization, asserting individual dignity and withdrawing from participation in a system that humiliates them" (Azodo, "Introduction" xxiv). Rama claims that Aissatou's friendship and sisterly bonding have helped her greatly. As she recounts her present and past conditions, she writes, "I feel no shame in admitting it to you" (68), highlighting through reflection a kind of healing process. Mary Jane Androne writes that "In the course of telling her story and the stories of other women and assessing their import in relation to Senegal past and present, Ramatoulaye also records the process of her own growth" (38). Moreover, Rebecca Wilcox further states that "Ramatoulaye performs an act of self-definition and self-analysis intended both for herself and for her confidante as she describes her feelings and reactions to the events in her life" (123).

Rama could not have undertaken this journey of self without the mirasse, an Islamic ritual performed at the death of a husband. Kenneth W. Harrow, in the introduction to the novel, defines mirasse as "the period of mourning and seclusion for widows, during which all the faults of the deceased are to be brought to light" (iv). Focusing on the negatives of the deceased is not necessarily the target of this seclusion. Following Harrow, I suggest that the mirasse opens a liminal space to self-reflection and enables Rama to reconfigure her life as a widow. Although Islam is not traditional to Senegalese Wolof culture, it has become the dominant faith among the Wolof. Wilcox argues that this period is significant to Rama's self-identification: "*Mirasse* becomes an avenue of empowerment for Ramatoulaye, who uses the time of her confinement to rediscover and recreate herself" (136-37). People from different backgrounds come to her house to pay their tributes—an act that shows how Rama is well positioned in her society and is highly respected.

Rama performs public grieving at the death of her estranged husband, Modou Fall, who died from a heart attack. As a Muslim, Rama performs the mirasse, whereby people come to commiserate with the bereaved. This Islamic ritual of mourning is carried out with the help of relatives, family, and friends. We get to know that her late husband Modou took a second wife, his daughter's best friend, Binetou. Little by little, readers get engrossed in an intimate world of lamentation: first, Modou's betrayal while he was alive, but during which time, Rama could not mourn openly, and secondly his death. Rama is a person who "bares her soul and divulges her innermost concerns, worries and beliefs" (Androne 38).

Rama extends beyond her ulterior appearance and goes on to achieve her full human potential. She transcends Modou's abandonment and embraces the fact that she, Rama, after all the sacrifices she has made, resembles "the cases of many other women, despised, relegated, or exchanged, who were abandoned like a worn-out or out-dated *boubou*" (Bâ 42). Nevertheless, despite her humiliation, she transcends her culturally determined position and the fate of widowhood and embraces her independence: She goes to the cinema alone, reads books, and listens to the radio in her spare time. Rama triumphantly overcomes her situation by clinging to her religion, family, and friends. She now feels empowered. Despite Modou's disgrace desertion, Rama does not give in to the pain or plot revenge as some women might do; she proves to be more than just an abandoned woman. She becomes a woman that exudes positivity and optimism.

Rama functions and is framed within the context of African motherhood practices: "My love for my children sustained me. They were a pillar; I owed them help and affection" (Bâ 55). Being a mother to twelve children, Rama unconsciously involves her offspring in whatever decisions she makes. At times, her children seem to act against her choices, especially the eldest, Daba, who represents the new generation and its questioning of old cultural beliefs. The occasional conflict of opinions that arise between Rama and her children is part of Bâ's illustration of how times have changed in Senegal, just like during Rama's youth when her French education made her look at her mother's ideas about love and marriage as quaint, and she refused to listen to her mother's advice. Hudson-Weems confirms that the "Africana womanist [is] committed to her family above all, and dedicated to the proposition of upholding the true legacy of the Africana woman as a strong, proud culture bearer" (*Africana Womanism* 96).

Rama does consider the prospect of walking away from her marriage, just as her friend Aissatou, another mother and a friend, had done earlier, but she is dissuaded from doing so because of her children and her acceptance of both her cultural and religious teachings about her role as a mother. To her, the best option is to stay married to provide a good example to her children that marriage is a constantly negotiable act of female self-sacrifice for the sake of the children. After all, she lived happily with her late husband; they were married out of love. She thought of the fate of others who took the path of divorce, as Aissatou had done. In Rama's specific situation, none of these options would be satisfactory: "I respect the choice of liberated women, I have never conceived of happiness outside marriage" (Bâ 58). It is true that Aissatou questions and rejects that kind of marriage that restricts woman to wifehood and motherhood alone. In her Mandingo-Wolof culture a woman has the right to leave a husband if she is unwelcomed by her in-laws; however, Rama, also a Western-educated woman, decides to stay with the husband that has betrayed their twenty-five years of marriage. She realizes that such an action would negatively affect a lot more people, especially her twelve children and her loving sister-aunties and mothers-in-law, who provide the type of friendship and community of mothers her society engenders. Her friend Aissatou never had any such support network even when she had two children for her husband. She did not find the support network of other women from her husband's family or friends. Yet Aissatou's and Ramatoulaye's reactions to motherhood and friendship reveal certain features of Africana womanism.

They address the multiple positions that contemporary individual Western-educated African women take in their societies when confronted with marital betrayals. Ada Azodo appropriates Donna Haraway's cyborg imagery to illustrate her definition of behavioural hybrid responses against totality: "Haraway demonstrates using the Cyborg, namely that we cannot lump all women into woman-as-one. Totality in the postmodern era, says Haraway, makes nonsense of women's particularities and individual voices" ("Theorizing" 68). The point here is to acknowledge and celebrate differences and confluences among women instead of homogenizing them and their problems under the context of some universalist feminist ideals. What sets local culture against foreign cultural ideals is that local African culture forms the roots of Africana women's identities, whereas foreign cultural ideals may in certain instances confuse those African women who unquestioningly embrace them in African spaces.

Rama starts her epistle by invoking her best friend, Aissatou, as a confidante in times of distress and/or happiness. Rama and Aissatou's friendship underscores Brandy Hayslett's contention that this type of sorority " empower[s] a woman, giving her the ability to change her life and those of others" (144). Hudson-Weems also clarifies and explains this relationship and details its nature in *Africana Womanist Literary Theory*: "Given the triple role that the Africana womanist must play—mother, partner, and breadwinner—it is very difficult to separate her personal and her professional world; thus, she needs that support system" (67). One can deduce that this type of solidarity is called for not just in times of distress but always.

Irène Assiba d'Almeida has argued that "Greater solidarity among women is needed to alleviate the agony women go through in polygamous situations" (164). I would dare say that sorority works in all situations whether polygamous or monogamous. What is important is that women should always have healthy avenues to express their feelings. Women are oppressed by cultural, class, and sexist paradigms. Bâ, thus, contemplates the different strategies to accommodate and ameliorate Western-educated Senegalese women's subordinate position in society. As Azodo writes: "The problems of women and men in Africa as due to a subordinated Senegalese (read African) subjectivity in the present where the new elite embrace a multicultural way of life that all but denies the legitimacy of traditional mores without becoming nonetheless the controlling centrality that is Western culture" ("Introduction" xi). This is partly true. Rama does not always allow her French colonial education to interfere with her native Wolof culture or with the principles of her childhood and Islamic religion, the sources of her strength and identification.

What sustains Rama on her journey of survival and self-recognition is her faith in female bonding. This allows her the space to meditate on her situation. Hudson-Weems writes the following:

> This sisterly bond is a reciprocal one, one in which each gives and receives equally. In this community of women, all reach out in support of each other, demonstrating a tremendous sense of responsibility for each other by looking out for one another. They are joined emotionally, as they embody empathic understanding of each other's shared experiences. Everything is given out of love, criticism included, and in the end, the sharing of the common and individual experiences and ideas yields rewards. (*Africana Womanism* 65)

Furthermore, Hudson-Weems goes on to clarify any mystification surrounding this kind of woman-to-woman relationship: "This particular kind of sisterhood refers specifically to an asexual relationship between women who confide in each other and willingly share their true feelings, their fears, their hopes, and their dreams" (65).

In Africana culture, female solidarity is introduced at an early age through mothers and grandmothers as well as at school. Here Rama relates the second spring of solidarity among women: "To lift us off the bog of tradition, superstition, and custom, to make us appreciate a multitude of civilizations without renouncing our own, to raise our vision of the world, cultivate our personalities, strengthen our qualities, to make up for our inadequacies, to develop universal moral values in us: these were the aims of our admirable headmistress" (Bâ 16). Rama is aware that as a Wolof woman, she is the bearer of her culture; she is proud of this and knows how to thwart any cultural alienation imposed by foreign structures she learns about in school.

Sisterhood in this context is based on mutual understanding of circumstances, as is demonstrated in the friendship between Rama and Aissatou. They are not just childhood friends; they have also had similar illusions of marriage as Western-educated women and experienced similar marital problems, albeit with different response choices. Aissatou chooses to divorce Mawdo, basically because she is driven away by her hateful and manipulative mother-in-law Aunt Nabou. In contrast, Aunt Nabou prefers to operate within the traditional Wolof caste system that marginalizes and persecutes people like Aissatou for her so-called lower caste origins. This leaves Aissatou with no option but to divorce Mawdo and leave. Rama opts to stay married to Modou because she is loved, respected, and supported by her in-laws, especially her sisters-in-law and mother-in-law. Being accepted and loved by them plays an important, if not a critical, role in Rama's commitment to staying in the marriage. Unfortunately for Aissatou, she has little room to manoeuvre; she has the terrible choice to either stay in a miserable marriage and be unloved and unwelcomed by Aunt Nabou, her mother-in-law, or to leave and start a new life. She chooses the latter—an action that should not be interpreted as feminist, or womanist, but as a pragmatic and culturally accepted and expected manoeuvre. Although Wolof tradition is patrilineal, women's rights are affirmed through the kind of power mothers wield in their families, especially with issues concerning inheritance. Thus, Aunt Nabou takes advantage of this and twists it to fit her agenda. She knows the extent of power she wields over her son and that the acceptance of her daughter-in-law depends on her. She consciously refuses to accept Aissatou because of her caste, which she believes is inferior to her son's caste. Thus, for both Rama, who marries a man within her caste system, and Aissatou who marries above her caste, dealing with their husbands' betrayals cannot be a uniform response. Rama swallows her hurt pride and stays in the damaged marriage, placing her children's interest above her grief, much like what Africana women, as Hudson-Weems theorizes, are driven to do. Rama acts within her society's expectations of a good wife and mother, thus assuring her survival and gaining her greater social prestige and respect.

Differences that exist between the two friends are dissolved by the strength of their bond, which Rama describes: "Forewarned, you, my friend, did not try to dissuade me, respectful of my new choice of life" (Bâ 48). In this respect, Aissatou's divorce is hailed by some Western feminist critics as the only viable solution, whereas they consider Rama's resolve to stay in her broken marriage an act of weakness—an affirmation of her internalized defense of female subordination. However, within a traditional African setting Rama's choice elevates her in the eyes of her society, "but for most women life in a polygamous marriage is far preferable to the social ostracism that they would have to face as unmarried women" (Olaussen 69), since women are taught that they should focus all their attention on their children and that patience and compromise are strategic techniques to hang on to if they want to survive as women. Androne even goes further: "It is important to see Ramatoulaye not as either conventional liberal feminist or conventional Senegalese woman of a privileged class, but as a woman forced to change because of the pressures of her experiences and who negotiates the problematic conditions of her life" (47). Rama's response does not automatically make Aissatou a Black feminist nor does it make Rama a radical Black African womanist. The truth of the matter is that Aissatou was left with no choice, for her mother-in-law did not accept her as a daughter-in-law. I emphasize the daughter because this single word holds a kind of bond that is supposed to replace the real bond between a mother and a daughter. A mother-in-law should be in place of a biological mother. This bond unfortunately is destroyed by Aunt Nabou, who never accepted Aissatou as part of her family. In Wolof societies, a woman is given the choice of either accepting to be a part of a polygamous marriage or to refuse it; as a matter of fact, it seems far preferable to stay in a polygamous relationship than be a single woman in these societies.

Through Rama, B advances motherhood, community, and friendship within theoretical and practical frames of negotiation, acceptance, self-discovery, recreative recuperation of memory, and respect for the struggles, achievements, and failures of traditional motherhood in her society, without rejecting other models of motherhood and community. Negotiation becomes a necessary theoretical frame to understand responses to patriarchy in Wolof society. In the novel, the principle of negotiation operates in connection to the different lines of action taken by Rama and Aissatou to deal with their marital problems. Negotiation implies flexibility and subsequently yields prospects for better futures for women. In Wolof societies, when a woman is rejected by her in-laws, she can either leave her husband and take her children or stay. When Rama thanks Aissatou for understanding her decision to stay with Modou Fall, she also says that she understands Aissatou's choice of leaving Mawdo, since the other option was to stay in a marriage that would only cause Aissatou despair and unhappiness.

Following this line of reasoning, including the story of Jacqueline in *So Long A Letter* is not a random narrative decision; it acts as a forewarning of the psychosocial effects on women in the absence of community and friendship. Jacqueline has no community of female friends in Senegal. She is marginalized both because she is Ivoirienne and Christian in a predominantly Muslim and Wolof society. Her husband's relatives alienate her because she refuses to convert to Islam. To complicate matters, her husband's reputation as a womanizer makes her a laughingstock, and she experiences marginalization: She is relegated and confined to the extreme margins of society. Her lack of contact with family or friends, or any bonding with other women, leads her to suffer psychological problems. Her neurologist explains to her: "You wish the conditions of life were different from what they are in reality, and this is what is torturing you" (47). Based on this diagnosis, Jacqueline leaves her husband to secure her wellbeing as well as her children's. Her position is unstable as her only tie to Senegal is her husband, whose religion and culture are alien to her. Jacqueline's brief story also helps to understand Aissatou, not from any feminist perspective but from a humanistic one. Had she stayed with Mawdo, she would have ended up mentally unstable like Jacqueline: "A nervous breakdown waits around the corner for anyone who lets himself wallow in bitterness. Little by little, it takes over your whole being" (Bâ 43). Jacqueline's story could be anyone's. Hence her presence in this story demonstrates how the absence of community and friendship among women who also happen to be mothers can result in psychological hardship for a mother.

Sisterhood, as formulated and performed in *So Long a Letter*, is not just based on mutual understanding or benevolence; it rests on the foundation of nonjudgment. Rama and Aissatou's friendship is an example of how friends tolerate and respect one another despite each having different approaches to life. Both were fortunate to find each other, yet they were also oppressed by the same community, which works towards destroying the lives of other women. Oftentimes, as I will show shortly, women's relationships can be determined and undermined by systems of control practiced by women over women. Such a lopsided type of woman-to-woman relationship is the opposite of what Hudson-Weems describes: "Women are the very foundation of life, whether they know it or not, and thus, they have to be a positive force in life for the ultimate survival of us all" (*Africana Womanist* 66).

Sisterhood affords them a haven of psychoemotional and material support (d'Almeida 161). For example, Aissatou gives Rama a generous gift, a brand new car. Additionally, towards the end of *So Long A Letter*, Rama refuses Daouda, a well-established doctor—a man who has been in love with Rama and who had proposed to her when she was eighteen. She had refused him back then, even though he had been the ideal choice of her mother, because she wanted to marry for love. Now a widow, Rama rejects Daouda's second proposal—a decision that is driven both by her pain of having had to share her husband and her decision not to do it to another woman because Daouda already has a wife. Rama's choices illustrate how Wolof women fight their cultural battles that pit women against each other or as Hudson-Weems calls it, "the phenomenon of female self-inflicted victimization" (*Africana Womanist* 73). In her act of refusing Daouda, Rama emotionally, ideologically, and socially empathizes her bond with Daouda's wife, even if it does not seriously undermine patriarchy and polygyny.

Azodo states that the ideal state of this bond is to "counter the effects of patriarchy and tradition" ("Introduction" xii)—that is, the intention is to raise awareness and elevate the status of African women. The idea of bonding among female subjects in the face of adversity is one that African women writers strongly advocate. Rama's action is a witness to the political as well as social transition happening in Senegalese society. This transition is generated by growing literacy and the dawning awareness among female subjects: "Now our society is shaken to its very foundations, torn between the attraction of imported vices and the fierce resistance of old virtues" (Bâ 76). Of course, these changes have their negative consequences, and women again seem to be at the receiving end of them.

Yet there are many Aunt Nabous. Rama describes Aunt Nabou as a woman who despite her lack of Western ideas about marriage, motherhood, sisterhood, and community interferes and uses her high traditional caste position to destroy her son's marriage and drive Aissatou to flee Senegal: "[Aunt Nabou] lived in the past, unaware of the changing world. She clung to old beliefs. Being strongly attached to her privileged origins, she believed firmly that blood carries its virtues, and, nodding her head, she would repeat that humble birth would always show in a person's bearing" (Bâ 26). These words reveal the callous caste-driven actions that so hurt Aissatou and undermined the optimism of Rama. Aunt Nabou is against Aissatou because she is the daughter of a goldsmith and, hence, of a lower caste. This generates and justifies Aunt Nabou's plot against her. We learn from Rama that Aunt Nabou suffered widowhood/abandonment and raised three children as a single mother, thus turning Mawdo into an overprotected son. However, this in no way justifies the humiliation and suffering she bestows on her daughter-in-law. Disrespectful of everybody's life, Aunt Nabou persuades her son Mawdo to marry his cousin, young Nabou, and inculcates in her both sexist and classist thinking: "Her aunt never missed an opportunity to remind her of her royal origin and taught her that the first quality in a woman is docility" (Bâ 30). Aunt Nabou undermines the social progress that Aissato and other Senegalese women have striven to achieve over decades. To Omofolabo Ajayi-Soyinka, Aunt Nabou belongs to the category of women who by their actions "help to sustain the patriarchy in power and further reinforce their marginalized status. It is in this sense that patriarchy controls women without seeming to" (163). By engaging patriarchal structures of the caste system, Aunt Nabou colludes with the constant undermining of female friendships and community bonding.

Someone like Aissatou, though lower on the caste ladder, refuses to succumb to her subordination thanks to her liberated sense of self, which was initiated through Western education. That is why she is hailed as a radical and a feminist; however, these critics fail to notice that Aissatou reacts to preserve her self-respect as a woman and a mother and that she is financially independent enough to take the action she takes. As Aissatou herself says: "Clothed in my dignity, the only worthy garment, I go my way" (Bâ 33). Aissatou is unwelcomed in her in-law's home, and she is thus left with no other choice but to leave, even if she becomes socially ostracized. Aissatou's final decision is in direct contrast to Maria Olaussen's idea of why women enter polygamous relations (69). The reader sympathizes with Aissatou's correct decision in divorcing her husband because she is a woman who places dignity above disrespect, her mind takes the rein of her heart. Living in a polygamous relation is a practice that she strongly refuses. Additionally, the many degrading words uttered by Mawdo—such as "You don't burn the tree which bears the fruit" (Bâ 32) or "A wife must understand, once and for all, and must forgive; she must not worry herself about betrayals of the flesh. The important thing is what there is in the heart" (Bâ 35)—asserts the wisdom of her decision and creates an empathetic understanding for her position. Most women would do the same as Aissatou if they were rejected by their mother-in-law or viewed in such an objectified manner.

What also empowers Aunt Nabou to act with impunity is the fact that elders are revered and respected in her society. In her description of elders, Hudson-Weems describes how their wisdom is indisputable because "they are the mother and fathers of [the] community" (*Africana Womanism* 70). In recounting Aunt Nabou's revenge, she details how Nabou's people received her: "Royally received, she immediately resumed her position as the elder sister of the master of the house. Nobody addressed her without kneeling down. She took her meals alone, having been served with the choicest bits from the pots. Visitors came from everywhere to honour her, thus reminding her of the truth of the law of blood" (Bâ 29). She already knows the extent of the power she wields around her; she manipulates her brother, son, and daughter-in-law. Aunt Nabou, the eldest in her family, as well as a grandmother, is captured in Mildred Lubin's words: "Grandparents were honored because it was believed that they were the closest to the ancestors, and the ancestors were important because they could assume revered status" (259). Thus, Aunt Nabou's immense power is derived from her society and the place of the mother/grandmother in the family. Aunt Nabou's case reflects how women further complicate their status in society and how they harm one another. Thus, the novel highlights all the healing Rama undergoes in her odyssey of emotional and spiritual restitution after being hurt both by her husband and by another woman.

It is often presumed that in times of grief, friendships and community play crucial roles in giving the grieving person much needed support. In Wolof society, this is so much more the case for widows. Women provide a community of comforters, helpers, comourners, and counsellors. Thus, Modou's funeral is teeming with crowds of female relatives, friends, and other community members who provide Rama with all the socioemotional and psychological support she needs. Scores of people, friends, and family members come to pay tribute to Rama: "What a seething crowd of human beings ... comes from all parts of the country, where the radio has relayed the news" (3-5). Modou's death frees Rama from the patriarchal hold he had over her. But in his death, both Rama and the rest of the female community feel a sense of relief and duty to commiserate with Rama even as they praise the dead body, which is culturally required. Yet their sympathy and support are with the resilient Rama. These facts are reflected in Rama's stream of consciousness "He rejected us. He mapped out his future without taking our existence into account" (Bâ 10). Pertinent to my argument is that the greatest amount of support Rama receives is from the sisters of Modou. They hardly pay any attention to Binetou and her gold digger of a mother. Retrospectively, Rama is happy that even although Modou had betrayed her, these same sisters and aunts remained her friends and family. They never abandoned her even when Modou was still alive, and they always spoke in her favour. Their friendship and company fortified her against the pain of divorce.

Sisterhood bonding is a community of women who share a bond of emotional, psychological, and social friendships through which they uphold and support one another. In the novel, this bonding is reflected in the relationship between Aissatou and Ramatoulaye. However, sisterhood is not a given, as seen in the destructive and self-serving interventions of Aunt Nabou. Genuine sisterhood, as reflected in the relationship between Rama and Aissatou, provides a workable coping mechanism for women in oppressive and abusive relationships. It strengthens women's resolve and helps them develop mental peace and dignity. Contemporary Africana women who enter into sisterhood relations provide the space for active social change in their respective societies. Instead of succumbing to despair and depression or assuming a victim mentality, the new Africana woman creates spaces for both individual and group development that are culturally relevant and socially uplifting.

In writing this letter to Aissatou, Rama creates her own intimate space to articulate her feelings and to claim her voice and agency. She subsequently becomes a self-assured and self-assertive woman who determines for herself how she wants to live her new life. Bâ invites the reader to witness the necessity of sorority—women's solidarity—as a site for sharing their own stories and their voices of wisdom as well as a support network to mitigate frustration and discomfort. In a heterosexist relationship, a woman must compromise, endure, be patient, and forget their subjectivity in multiple ways: "Both physically and emotionally abusive male-female relationships would decline significantly with the realization that women are now in support of each other rather than in opposition" (*Africana Womanist* 74). Thus, "Despite everything—disappointments and humiliations—hope still lives on within me. It is from the dirty and nauseating humus that the green plant sprouts into life, and I can feel new buds springing up in me (Bâ 94-95). Through sorority, Rama shows that women can and must support one another by sharing their pains, dreams, desires and frustrations in order to negotiate through levels of contradictions and oppressions within their societies as mothers, wives, daughters. In the process, they can provide one another with hope and healing. Bâ succeeds in envisioning African women's emancipation and empowerment.

Works Cited

Ajayi-Soyinka, Omofolabo. "Negritude, Feminism, and the Quest for Identity: Re-reading Mariama Bâ's *So Long a Letter*." *Emerging Perspectives on Mariama Bâ: Postcolonialism, Feminism, and Postmodernism*, edited by Ada Uzoamaka Azodo, Africa World Press, 2003, pp. 153-74.

Androne, Mary Jane. "The Collective Spirit of Mariama Bâ's *So Long a Letter*." *Emerging Perspectives on Mariama Bâ: Postcolonialism, Feminism, and Postmodernism*, edited by Ada Uzoamaka Azodo, Africa World Press, 2003, pp. 37-50.

Azodo, Uzoamaka Ada. "Introduction: The Phoenix Rises from Its Ashes." *Emerging Perspectives on Mariama Bâ: Post-colonialism, Feminism, and Postmodernism*, edited by Ada Uzoamaka Azodo, Africa World Press, 2003, pp. ix-xxxiii.

Azodo, Uzoamaka Ada. "Theorizing the Personal in Mariama Bâ's Novels: Narration as Configuration of Knowledge." *Emerging Perspectives on Mariama Bâ: Postcolonialism, Feminism, and Postmodernism*, edited by Ada Uzoamaka Azodo. Africa World Press, 2003, pp. 51-70.

Azumurana, Solomon Omatsola. "The Dilemma of Western Education in Aidoo's *Changes: A Love Story*, Naylor's *The Women of Brewster Place*, and Morrison's *Beloved*." *CLCWeb: Comparative Literature and Culture*, vol. 15, no.1, 2013, pp. 1-10.

Bâ, Mariama. *So Long a Letter*. Waveland Press, 2012.

d'Almeida, Irène Assiba. "The Concept of Choice in Mariama Bâ's Fiction." *Ngambika: Studies of Women in African Literature*, edited by Carole Boyce Davies and Anne Adams Graves, Africa World Press, 1986, pp. 161-71.

Harrow, Kenneth W. "Introduction." *So Long a Letter*, by Mariama Bâ. Waveland Press, 20212, pp. i-vi.

Hayslett, Brandy. "Sisterhood: Knowledge, Femininity, and Power in Mariama Bâ's *So Long a Letter*." *Emerging Perspectives on Mariama Bâ: Postcolonialism, Feminism, and Postmodernism*, edited by Ada Uzoamaka Azodo. Africa World Press, 2003, pp. 143-50.

Hill-Lubin, Mildred. "The Grandmother in African and African-American Literature." *Ngambika: Studies of Women in African Literature*, edited by Carole Boyce Davies and Anne Adams Graves, Africa World Press, 1986, pp. 257-70.

Hudson-Weems, Clenora. *Africana Womanism: Reclaiming Ourselves*. 1993. 3rd rev., Bedford Publishers, 1998.

Hudson-Weems, Clenora. "*Africana Womanism*: The Flip Side of a Coin." *The Western Journal of Black Studies*, vol. 25, no. 3, 2001, pp. 137-45.

Hudson-Weems, Clenora. *Africana Womanist Literary Theory*. Africa World Press, 2004.

Olaussen, Maria. "About Lovers in Accra: Urban Intimacy in Ama Ata Aidoo's 'Changes: A Love Story.'" *Research in African Literatures*, vol. 33, no. 2, 2002, pp. 61-80.

Wilcox, Rebecca. "Women and Power in Mariama Bâ's Novels." *Emerging Perspectives on Mariama Bâ: Postcolonialism, Feminism, and Postmodernism*, edited by Ada Uzoamaka Azodo. Africa World Press, 2003, pp. 121-42.

Chapter 10

"Can We All Stand Together and Agree on This?": Space, Place, and Mothering in Lauren Mills's *Minna's Patchwork Coat*

Hannah Swamidoss

In discussing studies in spatiality, Robert T. Tally Jr. notes the range of critical practices in understanding the role of space in literary studies. One of these is feminist spaces (5). With its engagement of geographical space and the subsequent placement of female agency, Lauren Mills's *Minna's Patchwork Coat* demarcates significant feminist spaces. Mills's narrative stays true to its historical setting and subsequently portrays the seeming limits of female agency as women stay within gendered roles. Although the text does not make any reference to separate spheres (nor does the author in her remarks about the book and the songs included in the text), the consistent expansion of the domestic sphere by the quilting mothers tests the rigidity of gender expectations.

Whereas Victorian domestic ideology initially tried to promote the value of women's contributions to society by emphasizing the importance of mothers and mothering, the concept of the domestic sphere also became a means to limit female agency, since women were expected to remain within its confines. Through their friendship and solidarity, the quilting mothers prove that the domestic space can have great influence in the public sphere. The ideas in the book tie in well with a feminist understanding of mothering as engaging with social and political change. In a review of key ideas in the development of the concept of mothering, for instance, Andrea O'Reilly observes that "Mothering freed from motherhood could be experienced as a site of empowerment, a location of social change" (3). Consequently, mothering as a feminist space in *Minna's Patchwork Coat* engages important political and social issues.

The historical setting places the book in the first wave of feminism, and although there is no mention of female suffrage, a different type of political engagement occurs in the narrative, which the novel's publication date of 2015 may explain. As Noëlle McAfee points out, third-wave feminists critique the overlooking of groups such as minorities and working-class white women, by first and second-wave feminists. The narrative demonstrates the importance of these overlooked groups through Aunt Nora, Minna's mother, and Minna herself and invests these characters (and the groups they represent) with a subversive form of agency. The subversive nature of this agency occurs through the flexibility and creativity of female agency when compared to male agency, the importance of the mother's place on female friendship, and the value the women see in narratives. Thus, I argue that *Minna's Patchwork Coat* through its engagement with geographical space and social place reworks the range and influence of mothers and mothering and presents mothering and female friendship as fundamental to social progress. As a novella for children, *Minna's Patchwork Coat* reveals and demonstrates to children the benefits of friendship in a diverse community of mothers. Such friendships are projected as the best way to build a future that is more equitable, inclusive, and fair.

Geographical Space, Male Agency, and Female Agency

The geographical space of Minna's Appalachian community requires hard physical labour, whether it is working in the coal mines, raising crops on the land, surviving the harsh winters, or protecting oneself from dangerous wildlife, such as bears and panthers. These aspects of the environment shape both male and female agency. The men, for instance, work the coal mines and do the majority of the work in raising crops and have the potential to thrive financially from both these endeavours. The land, however, also takes its toll on the men, particularly those working in the coal mines. Minna's father eventually succumbs to black lung disease, and the condition weakens him while he is still alive. Although the women do not work in the mines, they share the physical labour of the land and take care of the household. Women who live alone (such as the schoolteacher, Aunt Nora, or Minna's mother after becoming widowed) rely on themselves to work the land with limited help from the men of the community. After the father's death, male neighbours help Minna's mother with the plowing, fix the steps to the house, and give her a dog for protection from wildlife and strangers. Yet despite the seeming reliance of women on men, the narrative does not position male agency as superior to female agency; instead, the text portrays both genders having value, and the broadminded men of the community acknowledge the role of female agency within the community. Minna's father is an open-minded man. His presence in Minna's life marks the first half of the narrative. The father acknowledges and values female agency in various ways. Minna's father's love for his wife, Minna, and his son appears throughout this part of the narrative; he spends time with them and tries to take care of them to the best of his abilities. Additionally, Minna's father acknowledges the worth of female knowledge in the public sphere. The father recognizes Minna's need for schooling. He tries to provide a coat for Minna so that she can attend school, but he is unable to do so. This creates a critical opening for the women in the community to come together to save the situation.

This community of women referred to as the "quilting mothers" decides to help Lester attend school. They quilt the coat he needs to attend school but which his father is unable to purchase for him. Set in 1908 in a small Appalachian community, the narrative emphasizes that the women fully understand the potential consequences that Lester might face by attending school. The mothers, however, craft a plan in which Lester can unobtrusively attend school by helping the teacher with chores. When Lester's grandmother, Aunt Nora, expresses her fears that the men of their community will not accept these actions, one of the mothers exclaims that while the women will not stop mothering, they can stop "wifing" (Mills 206). The women agree to "stand together" and as Lester attends school, a new community begins to emerge through female wisdom, initiative, and agency (Mills 207).

The importance of the friendship and solidarity between the mothers pervades the novel. The quilting mothers help Minna attend school by sewing together the patchwork coat of the book's title, and the different patches help Minna negotiate the complexities of school. Consequently, domestic space plays an important role in the book. While the potency and potential of the domestic space become clear in the previous examples, it is important to note that the agency of the domestic space intersects with the geographical space of the Appalachians, which shapes the cultural aspects of the region and the community. Henri Lefebvre's distinction between physical and geographical space as well as social space and place proves useful in analyzing the types of agency that Mills's domestic space holds. Lefebvre argues that the abstract notion of space being empty does not account for how people value or utilize that space (3). In discussing social space, Lefebvre uses Venice as an example and argues that both the geographical space and how people utilize this space create Venice: "The space of the settlement on the lagoon, encompassing swamps, shallows, and outlets to the open sea, cannot be separated from a vaster space, that of a system of commercial exchange which was not yet worldwide but which took in the Mediterranean and the Orient" (76). Similarly, Mills's portrayal of the Appalachian environment reveals the intricate relationship between space and place. The land requires physical labour, whether it is in mining for coal or raising crops, which in turn shapes male and female agency. Likewise, the severe winters and the need for warm clothing can dictate whether a child attends school or not. In engaging with geographical space, the narrative demonstrates that female agency can transcend the domestic and shape the public sphere.

Another significant way in which the story uses Minna's father is to emphasize the importance of female agency. This occurs through his appreciation of Aunt Nora's knowledge of the land, particularly in taking care of livestock and knowing the medicinal value of herbs. By so doing, Minna's father (along with others in their community) places importance on a form of cultural knowledge that does not belong to the dominant white culture, since Nora's knowledge of plants and herbs stems from her Native American background. The father values this type of knowledge to the extent that he arranges for Minna to learn from Aunt Nora. When she teaches Minna the use of these plants, the older woman also passes on Native American traditions and beliefs, neither of which seems problematic to Minna's parents. Moreover, a subtle distinction occurs between how Western culture utilizes the land and how Aunt Nora does so. Although the narrative does not explore the negative aspects of the coal mining industry thoroughly, the narrative does depict Minna's father's work as disruptive to the natural order of things, a desecration of nature. It also brings death through lung diseases, which the men who work in the coal mines develop and die from. The father, for instance, loves bright colours because of the gloom of the mines. Likewise, he can breathe easier outside of the mines and loves the clean, fresh air. The mines also bring death through accidents and disease. Although the Native American way of life does not necessarily prevent death or disaster, the text portrays this lifestyle as more attuned to the land. By having Nora as the sole representative of Native American culture (Lester represents a mix of races: European American, African American, and Native American) in the story, the narrative associates this wiser understanding of the land with female agency. Aunt Nora, likewise, does not have the same gendered views about the natural environment that Euromerican women have; Aunt Nora has no fear of the bears and panthers and hunts animals. Through these various aspects, Minna comes to see female agency as natural and necessary.

The quilting mothers demonstrate flexibility at several levels. Although Minna's father does think innovatively, he tries to solve his problems on his own with less help from the community. For example, the father asks for Lester's help around the farm in exchange for reading lessons. Initially, this mutually beneficial arrangement may seem to mirror the quilting mothers' way of solving Minna's need for a coat or Lester's need for schooling. The quilting mothers have a wider network, including female family members in other states. This network constantly includes other people in society, such as Minna's teacher. Together, they think beyond customary ways and conceptualize collective solutions to their problems. When the mothers realize that there is no nearby school for children of colour that Lester could attend, they are undeterred. They transcend this institutional limitation and design a new solution. The mothers demonstrate that domestic space can expand into public space. Minna's father, in contrast, makes limited use of this domestic space, even though he values it a lot. For instance, he does not learn along with Minna (or from her) Native American knowledge and lore. Female agency asserts itself through mothering, female friendships, and female networking and can create and/or negotiate opportunities amid poverty.

Social Space: Mothering, Friendships, Inclusivity, Diversity, and Social Progress

The context of female friendships and social spaces presented in *Minna's Patchwork Coat* offers elements of critical interest. The book presents a range of social spaces from the market, church, school, to the homes of different characters, and all of these spaces provide opportunities for female friendship. Significantly, the narrative portrays the quilting mothers having strong healthy friendships while other female characters, like Minna's peers, must learn how to have such relationships. By having the mothers model and/or directly teach their children the value of friendship, the narrative emphasizes the importance of intergenerational mentoring of female friendships, particularly through mothering and creative use of the domestic space.

The narrative depicts the necessity of female mentoring by structuring a contrast between the mothers and their daughters. Whereas the quilting mothers value and help one another, the younger generation of Minna and her female peers need to learn how to establish such bonds. Girls around Minna's age, for instance, bully her when she finally attends school; the girls laugh at Minna's clothing and at her having to start at a lower grade. In this situation, Minna does have two good male friends, Lester and Shane, and the narrative also places importance on these friendships. Without diminishing the worth of Lester and Shane's friendships, the book represents the need for Minna to have female friends as well. To create these friendships, the story depicts the mothers intervening directly and indirectly in two key ways: through storytelling and Aunt Nora's unflinching support of Minna. The first occurs at Minna's house when Minna spends time with the quilting mothers. None of the mothers (except for Aunt Nora) know of the bullying that Minna endures at school. From other instances in the text, it becomes clear that the mothers and fathers quickly discipline their children's perceived inappropriate behaviour. Since the women are unaware of the hurtful behaviour of their daughters, they can provide a perspective of their children that Minna does not see or experience. The mothers supply this different viewpoint when they tell stories associated with the scraps of cloth that they contribute to Minna's coat.

Through these stories, Minna learns about the childhood experiences of her classmates. This storytelling of ordinary occurrences accomplishes different things. These tales humanize the other children for Minna; she no longer sees them only as bullies. This new perspective, however, is not meant to downplay or excuse the bullying that Minna experiences. Instead, this storytelling empowers Minna. She can, for instance, do what her peers cannot, which is to see others as more than one thing. Consequently, Minna affirms her self-worth— she is more than the clothes she wears or her academic grade level. The text shows something else of equal importance: Minna uses the mothers' stories about their children to find unusual ways of connecting to her peers. The mothers' storytelling provides a combination of direct and indirect ways of forming female friendships. The women, for instance, directly befriend Minna by allowing her to be a welcome part of the group even though she cannot yet sew. Moreover, Minna observes the camaraderie and solidarity between women and can understand and appreciate healthy female friendships. Consequently, Minna becomes empowered through the mothers' friendship in addition to their storytelling.

A more direct form of female intergenerational mentoring of friendship occurs when Aunt Nora listens to Minna's problems at school and offers her ideas and support to form friendships with the girls at the school. The narrative's depiction of Minna sharing her troubles with Aunt Nora instead of the other mothers (including Minna's mother) offers interesting elements. Since Lester is Minna's closest friend, Minna naturally confides in him and accordingly includes Aunt Nora when conversing with Lester. With her Native American background, Aunt Nora, however, also has a different type of social space than the Caucasian quilting mothers; Minna's experiences at school position her to identify with the marginalization that Aunt Nora and Lester experience daily. As a result, Aunt Nora's domestic space provides an enabling atmosphere for the development of female agency. This echoes bell hooks's notion of the homeplace. Rather than a disempowering place for marginalized and oppressed people, such as African Americans and Native Americans, the homeplace must be understood and interpreted as a place of resistance, enduring love, empowerment, and healing (hooks 41-50). Thus, storytelling is one of the ways of this empowerment. Through stories, not only does Nora give Minna lessons on how to navigate through the dominant European American culture but also teaches Minna many aspects of Native American culture that empower her. One of Aunt Nora's suggestions to Minna occurs when Nora realizes how much Minna would like to befriend one of the other girls. Nora proposes that Minna offer a gift to the girl—something that Minna holds dear to her heart, which will indicate the value of the friendship being offered.

Significantly, the narrative portrays Minna choosing a doll that she has made herself for the other girl to mother. The doll represents another form of the marginalized domestic space: the poor of the dominant culture. Minna's family barely makes ends meet, and her doll reflects this financial situation in the simple material of which it consists. Yet the doll also signifies the love, contentment, and happiness of the family in enjoying what they have and placing importance on relationships instead of money. Minna has a range of choices in which to make a toy and the fact that she chooses a doll that helps her mimic the healthy relationships of her family by mothering it speaks volumes. When Minna gives this doll to a much wealthier child, the doll represents the best of the domestic space of the poor and something of real worth to the other child. A strange dynamic follows: Even though the other child does not publicly display any liking for her new toy and seems to mistreat Minna's precious rag doll, she secretly treasures this gift. Minna, however, fails to understand the inner turmoil within this child. She then hastily asks for her doll back so that the doll will once again be loved. To do so, Aunt Nora counsels Minna to offer something of even more value than the doll—Minna's friendship. Although the other girl cannot immediately understand why Minna makes this request and certainly does not value Minna's friendship as equal in value, this exchange creates an opportunity later in the narrative for the two girls to discuss what happened during this incident. Of equal importance is that Aunt Nora goes along with Minna to the girl's house and supports her emotionally. Aunt Nora's marginalization by the dominant culture does not prevent her from intervening, offering support, and mothering and mentoring Minna as she learns how to form female friendships.

Several important ideas emerge from this type of mothering and intergenerational mentoring of friendship. The quilting mothers and Aunt Nora represent a range of ages, and although some of the women are young, the story demonstrates that women of any age enrich one another and society at large. Through this range of ages, the text stresses the importance of older women mentoring younger ones in the ways of friendship. Additionally, the narrative makes clear that friendship between women, even if not instinctive, can be learned and cultivated. The narrative makes the case that friendships between females benefit everyone. Minna's commitment to friendship empowers her to stand up to bullying in proactive ways, which even humanize the bully.

Since the story presents female friendships as vital to individuals and the community, the idea that women can create and actively participate in such friendships (albeit some with more effort than others) provides a potent form of female agency available to all. And although race and social class (represented respectively through Aunt Nora and Minna) present additional challenges to female friendships, these factors do not prevent such friendships from forming. These types of challenges instead lead to another interesting element: All adult mothers, for instance, must take risks to foster their mothering community, their families, and their communities. When the quilting mothers decide to help Lester attend school, no matter how secretive they are in the implementation of their plans, they know that they still risk being ostracized or worse. Of course, the risks faced by Lester and Aunt Nora are even graver, some of which they have already experienced.

While living in another part of the country, Lester's racially mixed parents were killed in a fire, which was most likely started by Caucasians motivated by racial hatred. Consequently, despite Lester's desire to try out the quilting mothers' plan, Aunt Nora still hesitates before she finally gives her consent. The quilting mothers demonstrate that they need to learn about and from one another. The European American mothers who belong to the dominant American culture must become aware of Aunt Nora's needs. Likewise, Aunt Nora must learn to trust the quilting mothers fully for Lester to attend school. More subtly, though, although Aunt Nora has been relegated to the periphery of the community, she has also chosen to remain in the periphery because of her desire to protect Lester from harm and her distrust of some of the community members. Through Aunt Nora and the willingness of the other mothers to perform these risks, a renegotiating of centre and periphery that moves Aunt Nora and Lester towards the center of the community's social space takes place and generates the beginnings of a potentially more inclusive and accepting society.

Tellingly, this renegotiating of who belongs where in these social spaces of this new community occurs through the creative use of the domestic space. The quilting mothers model a flexible approach to problem solving that fosters inclusivity, diversity, and social progress. When Aunt Nora teaches Minna the medicinal value of plants, she includes and welcomes Minna to take part in a different tradition. Similarly, this inclusivity and fostering of diversity can be seen when the mothers make a way for Minna and then Lester to attend school. The story also makes clear that the children (and adults) who are unkind to Minna and Lester should be addressed in hopes of restoration and not relegated to the margins of society. *Minna's Patchwork Coat* makes clear through its depiction of the domestic space that the prime social spaces of a community ought to have a place for all. Moreover, the different approaches female characters take to create a place for all demonstrate that careful thought and multiple strategies are needed for renegotiating social spaces. *Minna's Patchwork Coat* does not offer a simplistic panacea for societal ills but instead shows that the flexibility of the domestic space can offer the necessary solution for a situation. Consequently, the act of storytelling and the materiality of narrative seen in the patches of the quilt become of great importance.

"We Need to Know Each Other's Stories": Narrative, Physicality, and Social Space

The stories that the quilting mothers tell Minna as she chooses scraps for her coat frequently describe ordinary experiences, such as a child's love for a pet calf or fishing trips. Occasionally, a scrap of cloth will represent more dire circumstances, such as a premature baby struggling to survive. These stories, whether ordinary or unusual, not only offer Minna insight into her peers but also strengthen the bonds between the quilting. The narratives build empathy and compassion and demonstrate that no matter how different the mothers and their families are, they have similar concerns and can relate to one another. Narratives serve as sites for interdependent, healthy communities, as recognized by Minna's mom, who says, "We need to know each other's stories, so we'll know that on the inside we're all made up of dreams and fears and the same hope to be loved. If we all knew that, then we might know how to get along better" (Mills 266).

The physical, tangible aspects of the fabric—the distinct colours, texture, and wear and tear of each patch—are as much a part of the story as the narrative itself; a memory is quilted from the texture of the worn-out blanket that swaddled a premature baby or the sooty black cloth from Minna's father's shirt. As Minna retells the story of each patch, her classmates immediately want to touch the piece of cloth to reconnect with a childhood memory. Cloth touching is a ritual of healing and bonding among hurting children. After Lester tells his story, a boy who had earlier been rude to Lester asks him for permission to touch the patch of his quilted cloth that represents his narrative. The geographical space of the Appalachians is captured in the fabric; Minna appreciates how the wool and the odd feather mixed in with the wool represent "stories of the raspberry bush, the sassafras, the pine bark, the strawberry, the possum and rabbit, the mockingbird, and even old crow. All of their healing spirits would be inside my coat" (Mills 126). Listening to the stories, touching the patches, and feeling the softness of the stuffing, the children begin to "get along better" and create a new social space in which all their patches and stories have value for themselves and one another, sowing the seeds for friendship and community for years to come.

Conclusion

When considering mothering and female friendships, *Minna's Patchwork Coat* offers several points of critical interest. The book positions mothering as vital to a community, as it becomes a site for social progress and change. By using what Adrienne Rich in "When We Dead Awake..." calls "revisionary history," the use of storytelling and quilting become allegories of women's revisionary histories. Through them, the limits to female agency are removed. *Minna's Patchwork Coat* demonstrates that amid male domination of the public spaces and histories, women can still find creative ways to empower themselves through communities of mothers and friends. Through storytelling and quilting, these mothers also mentor the younger generation of females on using friendship and mothering communities to empower themselves and others. Considering the book's intended audience of eight-to-twelve-year-old readers, the narrative presents a valuable portrayal of an interdependent community in which there is a central place for all, regardless of gender, wealth, or race. Although there is a certain simplicity to the role of storytelling and mentoring in maintaining and creating female friendships, Mills does not offer a simplistic panacea to societal ills. Instead, the narrative offers creative solutions through friendships between mothers and in domestic spaces.

Works Cited

hooks, bell. *Yearning: Race, Gender, and Cultural Politics*. Routledge, 1990.

McAfee, Noëlle. "Feminist Philosophy." *The Stanford Encyclopedia of Philosophy*, 2018, plato.stanford.edu/entries/feminist-philosophy/. Accessed 27 Feb. 2022.

Mills, Lauren. *Minna's Patchwork Coat*. Little, Brown and Company, 2015.

O'Reilly, Andrea, editor. *Feminist Mothering*. State University of New York Press, 2008.

Tally, Robert, editor. *Teaching Space, Place, and Literature*. Routledge, 2018.

Yalom, Marilyn, and Theresa Donovan Brown. *The Social Sex: A History of Female Friendship*. Harper Collins, 2015.

Chapter 11

Chinese Mothers Creating a Community of Maternal Support

Catherine Ma

Women who are great moms make the best kind of friend.

—Teddy Cornell (my friend since 1989)

Being a mother of three, it was important to me to find a community of mothers who shared a cultural understanding of the trials and tribulations of being a Chinese mom. Other cultures do not admonish a woman for eating watermelon while pregnant or expect them to eat pig's feet made with ginger and black vinegar after she gives birth.[1] To share a mutual understanding of these cultural norms fosters a unique sense of community that is quite rare yet so needed. Motherhood has always been challenging for me but having a close-knit community of friends who are also moms has been my saving grace. When I first became a mother, I quickly learned how isolating motherhood was, which seemed ironic for two startling reasons: I was never alone having to care for a tiny new human, and no one ever mentioned how lonely motherhood could be. Learning these harsh realities angered me as I felt duped and hazed at the same time. When I ventured out into the world as a new mother to Gymboree and Mommy & Me classes, I quickly learned that there were two kinds of "mom friends," or friends who are also mothers. There is the mom who always speaks about how perfect motherhood is, describes it as the ultimate calling for all women, and can talk all day about the benefits of Clorox wipes. These are not my people. I found motherhood extremely exhausting and often unfair. (How come my career was put on hold while men's careers soared from parenthood?) Breastfeeding also hurt like hell. I recall asking out loud, "Why can't the milk come out of my elbow?!" Many times I just wanted to survive until the end of the day.

I tried being the mother who thought motherhood was perfect, but it was too much for this outspoken and sometimes salty New Yorker. When I expressed my displeasure at the injustices of newfound motherhood, some mothers would look at me as if I were a leper, so I learned quickly to silence my voice. There was a short time when I thought I was the problem. Maybe I just needed to suck it up, play along while sharing recipes (I also do not enjoy any facet of cooking), and tout the benefits of Clorox wipes? Maybe this is what motherhood is all about? Maybe I needed to change myself to make these my people?

It took me a while, but I finally found the other type of mom who had her dreams to fulfill that had nothing to do with motherhood and parenting. She is angry about the injustices of mothering and outspoken regarding the monotony of caring for little people. It is not that she hates being a mother; instead, she seeks to balance the trials of motherhood with her dreams and aspirations. And honestly, for a while, it seemed as though these women were like magical unicorns: You knew of their existence, but you never met one in real life.

My Magical Unicorn

I was still a graduate student when my husband and I started our family, and I was the first among my peers and family to have a baby. Because I changed my dissertation topic to breastfeeding ideology, my doctoral advisor recommended that I speak to one of her more advanced students who was also a mother, and we set up a day to meet. The first question she asked seemed to be a vetting question, how was I finding motherhood? I found myself at a crossroads: Do I tell her the truth, or do I ramble on about how great Clorox wipes are? My pointed reply was "It's kicking my ass." The courage to be truthful had a domino effect, and she came forward with her truth. Her second-year doctoral exam was about banal maternalism, which focused on the silences that revolved around motherhood. Reading her paper, I knew I had found my people. She introduced me to the "motherhood mystique," in which motherhood is considered a woman's primary source of fulfillment and mothers are called to embrace being the sole caregiver and nurturer for their families (Green 191; Macdonald 16; Skott 1487). The motherhood mystique often left me feeling as though I was suffocating and drowning, yet I still fell into the trap of trying to fit myself into that restrictive model. Eventually, my defining moment in motherhood was finding this graduate student; she was my saviour, my comrade, my people. Our fateful meeting was evidence to me that I was not crazy for feeling what I felt or for what I knew to be true for me. This is not to say that mothers cannot be excited about Clorox wipes. We all have to mother in our own way and are each entitled to mothering in the way we deem best.

What my colleague taught me is that there are a multitude of ways to mother; likeminded mothers are out there, and I could still hold on to who I was before I became a mother. These valuable lessons helped foster my confidence as a mother, and as my confidence grew, I felt less of a need to judge others and became more forgiving of myself. This helped me understand the degree of animosity and judgment among mothers. I have now become more adept at separating myself from other people's drama. I listen with a sympathetic ear, gently remind my mom friends to not become entrenched in other people's drama, and to use that opportunity to practice stepping away. I cannot speak for others, but once I made that decision for myself, motherhood became less stressful, as I was able to focus more on building community with the mothers I choose to become friends with.

The Need for This Literature

One thing I quickly noticed was the lack of published research on the development of friendships between Chinese mothers, which makes this topic even more pressing. It is almost as if Asian maternal friendships do not exist in a research setting. I was able to find writings on maternal friendships in blogs and other forms of informal writing, but they were largely about friendships in the white, upper-middle-class stratum. One article from *Parents* magazine listed six steps on how to make mom friends, which included the following: 1) Put yourself out there; 2) make the first move; 3) get contact information; 4) plan the first play date; 5) utilize naptime as a play date; and 6) confirm the connection (Straker Hauser). I could not help but chuckle at the resemblance of these steps to dating. Other articles discussed the difficulties in finding mom friends because mothers are the most judged group of individuals, and it may be difficult for other mothers to quell the constant judgment that surrounds motherhood and mothering (Lang). The articles I found most validating discussed the value of mom friendships that emphasized the particular strengths of friends who remind you that the difficulties of parenting young children are only temporary, that you were once an interesting person before you became a mother who may not have time to shower, and that it is acceptable to want to beat up the kid who is picking on your kid (as long as you do not follow through) (Robinson).

My Circle of Friends

I live in a conservative neighbourhood in New York City that does not value diversity, which has made me more appreciative of the friendships I've had with other Chinese mothers throughout different stages of my life and career. In our tight-knit community of Chinese moms, we can vent about culturally relevant issues that only other Chinese moms can understand. We have laughed out loud about and/or commiserated over negotiating the difficulties of intragroup discrimination that are based on your dialect; raising children who are both Chinese and American; balancing Chinese and American values in the home; and navigating our way through the murky waters of Chinese mothering. Raised in a traditional Chinese household, my mother often told me that I was selfish and had a bad attitude. While enjoying lunch with my Chinese mom friends, we share stories of being labelled as having a bad attitude as children and laugh about the different Chinese euphemisms that were used to describe our bad attitudes. Over the years, our parents had told us that we would never find a husband who would put up with us. Needless to say, we all married strong men who were more than happy to put up with our bad attitudes. These commonalities bind us together as friends and preserve our mental health, all with a good and hearty laugh. This chapter focuses on my friendships with five of my dearest friends who have journeyed with me into motherhood. Each of these phenomenal women has taught me so much about myself, helped me weather storms, and celebrated achievements that could not have been reached without their support. I could not have survived motherhood without my sister-in-law, Maria, childhood friend, Josephina, colleague, Lili, and two retired pharmacists, Eileen and Agnes, who had been best friends for many years before including me in their tribe.

I have a healthy fear of Maria as she is a no-nonsense type of individual. I have always been a tad afraid of saying something that may piss her off, but as I have gotten to know her over the years, I realize what a strong ally she is to not only me but everyone she is close to. My respect for her is based on her generosity and how she has been there for my children since the day they were born. She has gone to every one-month baby banquet (infant mortality used to be high in China, and many infants did not survive to their first month of life, so only infants who reached this one-month milestone were celebrated with a multicourse meal with the entire extended family) for each of my children, school function for special person breakfast, and has rearranged her vacation schedule to attend their birthday parties. She picks them up from school when I am at work, and I am confident that my children are always in good hands when she is around. She is the fun aunt who never scolds and always loves. Anyone who treats my children with the utmost respect will always garner my utmost respect.

I met Josephina when I was just nine years old, and, fatefully, we found each other again as mothers. Unknown to us, my husband's aunt, who had recently emigrated from China in 2004, was hired as their nanny. One day when I took my children to the park, I recognized her and asked if she was the Josephina from our summer day camp days. We quickly became reacquainted; our children were of similar ages, and we both spoke Cantonese. Some days, it is refreshing to speak in one's native language, as it reinforces cultural ties that seem so critical in today's political climate. Josephina is like the Chinese mayor; she knows so many Chinese people and is an active member of the Chinese community in our borough. She teaches me to be more mellow when I am a little too outspoken and salty.

Lili is my dear frolleague (friend + colleague) who took the initiative to contact me from the email list after we found out we were both chosen for a prestigious fellowship. I was a new tenure-track psychology professor who was acclimating to teaching a heavy load and settling in my new department. Little did I know how few tenure-track professors were Asian. According to the 2013 National Center for Education Statistics, the odds are not in my favour, as Asian female assistant professors made up a paltry 1.05 per cent of all professors, and the statistics continue to be more dismal at the associate and full professor levels at 0.73 per cent and 0.44 per cent, respectively. She told me that there was only one other tenure-track Chinese professor at our college. Lili has been such an avid supporter of my accomplishments, and we often spend so much time laughing in each other's offices that other colleagues have to tell us to simmer down because it sounds like we are having too much fun. She has also taught me so much about my Chinese heritage, Chinese feminism, diaspora, and ethnic pride.

Eileen and Agnes formed their friendship long before I came into the picture, but their willingness to include me in their circle is what makes them so special. I have been participating in a weekly yoga class at the local YMCA for well over a decade; six years ago, an older Chinese woman invited me to lunch after class. That is how I met Eileen who is one of the most outspoken Chinese women I have ever met; immediately, I felt like I had met myself from the future. Ironically, she wrote in my Christmas card that I reminded her of a younger Eileen. She is also one of my funniest friends, and our weekly postyoga lunches, joined by her best friend, Agnes, are filled with laughter. Eileen and Agnes bonded as best friends and as the only two Chinese pharmacists working on Staten Island, New York City. The support they offered each other helped them and their families thrive through busy and sometimes difficult times. I love spending time with both of them, and the similarities we find among the three of us are uncanny. Their husbands are from my husband's and Maria's hometown in China, whereas Agnes is from Hong Kong like me. One day as we were eating lunch, I noticed that Agnes and I had the same wedding ring design. The odds of that are astronomical.

The generosity of these two women in accepting me into their tribe and sharing their wisdom has enriched my life in so many ways. Eileen said it the best when she stated that I keep her young and her wisdom keeps me wise. To have more experienced friends offers me a unique perspective that my same-age peers do not. Eileen and Agnes ground me when naiveté is present, and they offer an outlet in discussing issues that I do not feel comfortable discussing with others. Their generosity in sharing their wisdom with me has helped me grow and deal with conflicts in a more positive light.

Except for Josephina who has a more traditional work schedule, the rest of us meet weekly for lunch, as we have more flexibility in our schedules. It takes a bit of juggling to find a day where we are all free, since we are busy with our families, children, grandchildren, publishing, conducting research, writing, elder care, and the millions of other tasks related to running our households. One thing for certain though: We all look forward to our lunch dates and to sharing news, funny stories, and advice. This sense of community feeds our souls, and we savour our three-hour luncheons as an opportunity to relax and see ourselves as individuals.

Great Friends Share the Greatest Life Lessons

Some of the best life lessons that have defined true friendship to me, I have learned from this group of friends. Maria offers us some perspective on facilitating friendships among women in China. She was born in Guang Dong province in the Guijing Township, located in southeast China, and recalls the strong community support for mothers in her town growing up. When she was a child, it was a common practice in her village to place newly married women in a group with other fairly new brides to work in the rice fields or have new mothers grouped to work with other new mothers. In this way, many women became lifelong friends. This way of forming friendships is different in the United States, as she noted, "It's extremely difficult to find time to even make friends with your neighbors because every family is busy with their own agenda and schedules." Experiencing these contrasts, Maria truly values the closeness of family and friends. Seeing how she treats her two brothers and how they treat one another has taught me a new way of viewing siblings.

Although I am her sister-in-law, she treats me as a sibling. We are invited to her house for elaborate dinners, special occasions, or for no reason at all; she always cooks my children's favourite dishes and often invites them to cook with her; my children love doing things with their auntie. My youngest is a picky eater, and she accommodates his palate every time we eat at her home. My older son will eat anything under the sun, and she always makes sure he has plenty to fill his bottomless stomach. My oldest daughter loves her gourmet dishes that I never have the time or patience to make. When I come home from a long day at work, I often find prepared meals in my fridge that she took the time to not only cook for us but also deliver to us. She knows how dreadful I find cooking and helps in any way she can. We also share a similar level of saltiness, which is a combination of assertiveness with a touch of snarkiness. She teaches me how to be a better daughter through her example. Maria inspires me by advocating for her elderly parents and takes on the majority of all their elder care needs. The sacrifices she makes for our family are indicative of the integrity she holds. What I know about Maria is that she has a kind heart and will always stand up for the people she loves. I can always count on her to have my back, and because of that, I will walk through fire for her.

Josephina shares sisterly qualities similar to Maria. When our children were younger, it was nice to have someone to meet up at the playground and enjoy a day at the park. Her generosity puts mine to shame, but I think we complement each other well: she teaches me how to be more accommodating, and I teach her how to be less accommodating. Since she was thirteen years old, she has worked and brought home a paycheck; adopting the life of a stay-at-home mom altered her world. I helped her realize that her unpaid labour as a mom was just as, if not more, important to her family. Our friendship reminds us that we are not merely someone's mother but a person who still holds value as an individual with outside interests. This multiplicity of identities salvages our sanities by buffering the stress associated with motherhood and reminding ourselves that we are more than just mothers (Thoits 183-84). Referring to the importance of mom friendships, she valued having "someone in my corner, with similar backgrounds and similar upbringing giving me validation that I am not a failure." We sometimes need a cheerleader to remind us that tomorrow is another day and another opportunity to make different choices. Her activism and community service have shown me the value of becoming more civically engaged in my community; I am always amazed at her networking skills and her ability to foster ties with the influential Chinese people in our borough. She is also always willing to lend a helping hand. One time, my laptop was infected with a virus, and I panicked because I had not backed up any of my work and all my dissertation research was on the hard drive. I called Josephina to ask her husband, who is a computer specialist, if he could salvage anything. She came to my house to pick it up and not only did her husband disinfect my computer and save all my data, but they refused to accept any payment from me. Her brothers with their families are also very kind to my children, taking the time to remember their names and making them feel so welcomed.

Sometimes work can be a hassle, but if you are lucky and I mean truly lucky, you may find a frolleague who makes it a joy to go to work. This is who Dr. Lili Shi is to me. We have so much fun just laughing together. A frolleague is someone with whom you can talk about work, and they understand exactly what you are talking about. There is no need to explain work dynamics, the trials of teaching an almost ridiculous teaching load of nine courses per year, going up for tenure, promotion, etc. She knows what needs to be done, and we support each other in reaching our work goals, which is of utmost importance given that our racial group makes up less than 0.5 per cent of the faculty body at our college. She makes coming to work so much more fun, and we have even presented at conferences together. Having that camaraderie is special. She taught me about linguistic currency, in which speaking Cantonese (my dialect) does not offer the same perks as speaking fluent Mandarin, which is her native dialect. I love going with her to any Asian place, and she will speak Mandarin with the resultant effects of receiving the best service among other perks while being treated like queens. Her eloquence in describing the value of mom friendships is found in this statement:

> Our shared moments of maternal frustrations and triumph, our everyday trials and tribulations as immigrant tenure-track junior faculty, our connected affective terrains where we claim our feelings growing up Chinese and becoming Chinese mothers, occupy such important space of feminist and womanist solidarity that grounds and nurtures my core identity of being a Chinese feminist academic mom.

Her feminist ways also help me become more civically engaged.

When I first met Eileen, I knew we would be good friends. I have always listened to my intuition when it comes to friendships. It is difficult to describe, but I just know upon meeting a stranger whether I will become close friends with that person. I do not have many older

Chinese female friends, so it was interesting for me to connect so deeply with Eileen. We share a belief in karma as evident in her quote: "The more connected we are, the better we feel. The better we feel, the healthier we are. That is a win-win situation." I recall her sharing how she asked God and the universe to send her someone smart and interesting, approximately a year before our paths crossed. She is passionate about gun control, which also fuelled my civic engagement in my community.

I also learned a valuable lesson from Eileen, who disclosed to me that she is prone to depression. Being a psychologist, I found this interesting as I am aware of the stigma surrounding mental health issues in society and even more so among the Chinese population. I asked her if she felt that people from her hometown in China were prone to depression, and she believed it was a characteristic of her people. She told me how she actively fights against her depression, and because she recognizes this in herself, she can control it by surrounding herself with people who do not have negative attitudes or are constant complainers. I asked her for advice regarding others who also suffer from depression but due to cultural factors are not open to seeing a therapist or talking about past trauma. I felt helpless and guilty that being a psychologist, I was unable to help this person, but she reassured me that certain generations do not see the value of seeking therapy, and that is just the way they are, but one thing I could do was to make sure that their emotional climate was light with a touch of silliness to keep their mood less dark. That made a lot of sense to me, and it was certainly something I could do because I come from a long line of funny Chinese people, and Eileen can easily attest to that fact. I am learning that the best types of friends are the ones with whom you can laugh with but also discuss deeply personal issues and offer sage advice. Our discussion helped me gain a new perspective on the role of mental health in a much stigmatized community that often feels a great degree of shame in acknowledging mental health issues. Eileen also introduced me to her best friend, Agnes.

Agnes is retired with grown children my age but still very much young at heart. We share similar beliefs about maternal friendships. As Agnes said, "Every mom, young or old needs friends. We need friends to share happiness, support, and comfort you during difficult times." Shortly after we met, her husband needed an organ transplant. Since it was close to Chinese New Year, I gave her a lucky red envelope, or a "hong-bao," with some money that had a Chinese saying to wish him good health. That simple gesture touched her because Chinese people are somewhat superstitious when it comes to health problems, so sending a little wish for good health during a health crisis was considered especially fortuitous during the new year. As I got to know more about Agnes, I realized how our lives shared so many stark similarities, such as growing up on the Lower East Side, frequenting certain neighbourhoods, such as Essex Street in Manhattan or Mays department stores, harbouring similar fears of living without our husbands, relying on them maybe a little too much, hating insects, and driving by ourselves. Because we shared so many similar fears, I knew how to help alleviate her fears by telling her that everything was going to be alright, offering to come over to kill her bugs, and reminding her to take care of herself so she can continue taking care of others. Some times having someone listen to your fears and share some comforting words is enough to ease your burden and Agnes's statement "Talking with my friends would relieve my stress, especially during the time my husband was sick" epitomizes that sentiment.

Seeking Mom Friends

Some days I wonder to myself, how did I get so lucky to be surrounded by so many phenomenal women? I truly feel blessed to have such a wide variety of friends who complement my strengths and weaknesses so well. In looking at myself, I think it has a lot to do with knowing who I am as an individual, woman, mother, sister, daughter, and, most importantly, friend. I feel being born in the Chinese astrological year of the pig is an asset because pigs make great, loyal, and funny friends. Eileen has often said how much nicer it is to have friends who can laugh out loud. Agnes also agrees that being able to laugh together is a great way to relieve stress. The trials of motherhood are real, and there are times when going through the daily routine of being a mother, one forgets about self-care, which is vital to perform all the acts of mothering.

To be able to have a dear friend who helps make the mundane tasks of mothering more bearable is truly a gift. As women get older, the importance of friendships becomes more apparent. Research by Jason Newsom and Richard Schulz found that older adults need that social connection with others to ward off impairment in quality-of-life variables as well as depression (34). Agnes finds it easier to make friends now that she is older and feels that all moms can greatly benefit from supportive friends. Her words ring true, as friendships among elderly women show a preventative effect against depression and loneliness, which are critical factors in maintaining a long and healthy life (Aday, et al. 68-69). Steve Duck might have said it best: "Friendships do not start until people do friendly things in friendly places: they are not created merely by friendly talk" (56). In other words, one must know how to be a friend to have friends. Friendships where individuals share the same race and ethnic background also offer a buffer to the macro- and microaggressions people of colour often face that negatively affects their health through the accumulated stress of daily acts of sexism, racism, and discrimination (Sue, et al. 279). I can personally attest to the benefits of sharing my experiences of racist encounters and having a supportive network of women who can readily understand and empathize with their own lived experiences. To have those shared experiences, albeit negative, helps preserve my sanity, as I have my experiences validated. As Josephina noted, "When we go through different stages of school, activities, and life in general, it is reassuring to have someone to bounce ideas off of." It is that support that helps me power through another day and enables me to recharge.

Through each of my mom friendships, I have become more secure in how I see myself, which in turn facilitates my ability to become a more compassionate, understanding, and better friend. These women have taught me so much about life and the value of having not just one but multiple meaningful friendships. In reflecting on each of my friendships with these amazing women, I realized that I am the common link between all of us, and that realization fills me with a great sense of awe that destiny brought our paths together. It has made me recognize the importance of fostering community among women and especially mothers. I unknowingly became the person responsible for bringing together so many wonderful moms, and I know how grateful we all are for this synchronicity. When it comes to building community, we should all take a step outside of our comfort zones and ask another mom out to lunch, offer a friendly compliment to a mom who looks like she is having a difficult day, or be an active listener to a mom who needs someone to talk to. Motherhood can be isolating at times, and to know someone who has walked in your shoes can make the tribulations of mothering more bearable and even fun at times. That is what true maternal friendships are all about.

Endnotes

1. In keeping a balance of hot and cold, watermelon is considered too cold and believed to increase miscarriage, whereas pig feet made with ginger and black vinegar supposedly helps a mother's milk flow.

Works Cited

Aday, Ronald, Gayle Kehoe, and Lori Farney. "Impact of Senior Center Friendships on Aging Women Who Live Alone." *Journal of Women & Aging*, vol. 18, no. 1, 2008, pp. 57-73.

Auyeung, Agnes. Personal interview. 3 May 2018.

Chin, Josephina. Personal interview. 26 April 2018.

Chu Walters, Maria. Personal interview. 30 September 2018.

Cornell, Teddy. Personal interview. 10 December 2018.

Duck, Steve. *Relating to Others*. Chicago, Dorsey Press, 1988.

Green, Fiona Joy. "Re-conceptualizing Motherhood: Reaching Back to Move Forward." *Journal of Family Studies*, vol. 21, no. 3, 2015, pp. 196-207.

Lang, Rebecca. "The Real Reason It's So Hard to Make Mom Friends." *Motherly*, mother.ly/love/why-is-it-so-hard-to-make-mom-friends. Accessed 18 Feb. 2022.

Macdonald, Cameron. "The Rise of the 'Motherhood Mystique'." Feminism and Families Today: What's the New Mystique? A Council on Contemporary Families Feminine Mystique Symposium, 18 February 2013, University of Miami School of Education and Human Development, Miami, FL. Conference Presentation.

Newsom, Jason, and Richard Schulz. "Social Support as a Mediator in the Relation Between Functional Status and Quality of Life in Older Adults." *Psychology and Aging*, vol. 11, no. 1, 1996, pp. 34-44.

Robinson, Holly. "The Importance of Mom Friendships." *Parents*, 29 Jul. 2015, parents.com/parenting/moms/the-importance-of-mom-friendships. Accessed 18 Feb. 2022.

Shi, Lili. Personal interview. 8 February 2018.

Skott, Beth Pamela. "Motherhood Mystique." *The Wiley Blackwell Encyclopedia of Family Studies*, edited by Constance Shehan, John Wiley & Sons, Inc., 2016, pp. 1487-89.

Straker Hauser, Wendy. "6 Ways to Make Mom Friends." *Parents*, 29 Jul. 2014, parents.com/parenting/relationships/friendship/making-mom-friends. Accessed 18 Feb. 2022.

Sue, Derald Wing, et al. "Racial Microaggressions in Everyday Life. Implications for Clinical Practice." *American Psychologist*, vol. 62, no. 4, 2007, pp. 271-86.

Thoits, Peggy A. "Multiple Identities and Psychological Well-Being: A Reformulation and Test of the Social Isolation Hypothesis." *American Sociological Review*, vol. 48, no. 2, 1983, pp. 174-87.

To, Eileen. Personal interview. 20 May 2018.

Chapter 12

Beyond DNA

Janice Tuck Lively and Mary Barbara Walsh

Janice and Mary in One Voice

We, Janice and Mary, became friends late in life, after our mothers' deaths and as our children stumbled towards and through adulthood. Our friendship began as a function of our work but quickly transformed to centre around shared elaborations of the struggles and the joys of mothering. Despite profound differences regarding race, marital status, and disposition, we discovered an affinity in terms of our experiences of mothering and being mothered. Together, we reflected on and digested our experiences and together we struggled with our ongoing challenges as mothers. There are things about mothering that only become apparent during the sharing of our experiences: mutual care and vulnerability as well as friendship. By sharing our experiences, our friendship eased, just a bit, the anxiety attendant to motherhood and enhanced, just a bit, the joy possible in mothering. Beyond friendship, we found our community of support, comfort, and encouragement. We intend to offer a glimpse into that community and to share what we learned about mothering through the lens of our friendship.

In more academic terms, in this chapter, we engage in the process of reciprocal dialogue as a means of grappling with various representations of mothering. Through this reciprocal dialogue, we hope to provide space for the expression of our unique narratives as well as the possible emergence of a shared narrative regarding mothering. In 1999, Maria Lugones and Elizabeth Spelman proposed reciprocal dialogue as an approach to feminist theory as it "does not reduce each one of us to instances of the abstraction called 'women'" (486). Reciprocal dialogue demands that we, Janice and Mary, each alternatively position ourselves throughout this chapter as an insider and as an outsider, listening and inquiring in a spirit of engaged friendship and genuine sisterhood. We invite our readers to do the same—not to look for answers, definitions, or directions but rather to share in the process of listening and learning.

To engage representations of mothering beyond our own, we also incorporate a process of call and response. In this case, the representations of mothering act as the call for our reciprocal responses. According to Maggie Sales, the call and response process "depends upon the repeated interaction of the one and the many" (43) and allows the meaning of the exchange to evolve in and through the process. In this way, meaning is neither stagnant nor monolithic but rather communal, multiple, and evolving. Importantly, the call and response process represents an ongoing process that ultimately ends with a call to continued engagement and exchange. We hope that this chapter represents one moment in the evolving exchange regarding mothering.

I. From the Start . . .

It's well known that the transfer of mitochondrial DNA from mother to offspring, often called maternal inheritance, occurs in humans.... You inherited your mitochondrial DNA from your mother, who inherited hers from her mother and so forth. Maternal inheritance also gave rise to the idea that there exists a "Mitochondrial Eve," a woman from whom all living humans inherited their mitochondrial DNA.

—Steph Yin

Mary's Voice

If you were to play a game of "one of these things is not like the others" with my mother, my sisters, and me as the prompts, I would be designated as the odd daughter out every time. My mother, a graceful, slender blonde gave birth to four tall, blonde daughters—and me, a stubby, brown-haired throwback to someone earlier in the chain of DNA or perhaps to my father's heartier stock. How I envied the long-legged, freckle-less bodies of my mother and sisters. But my siblings and I all share blue eyes, inevitably so, given that both our mother and father were blue eyed. Through these blue eyes, we can trace our heritage—my mother's, my siblings', and my own—back to a smallish, damp green island just off a bigger, imposing island across the Atlantic Ocean. To this day, if I close my eyes and try to remember the physical reality of my mother, it is her soft blue eyes I remember best—eyes that did not probe, or interrogate, but rather that drew me in and held me in their sweet, warm glow.

Janice's Voice

From as far back as I can remember, I was always told that I looked just like my mother, who in turn looked like her mother. Our bodies were lean and slim with just enough derriere to make them interesting. Our features tended to be like those of many Black women: full lips as well as the Nubian nose commonly found in those of African descent—a longer bridge and wider nostrils, large expressive brown eyes, and skin tones in varying shades of brown. Within three generations, we had three distinct skin tones: mine was café au lait; my mother's was cinnamon brown, and my grandmother's was a warm chestnut. Based on cultural standards at the time, there was nothing exceptional about our beauty through the genes we passed from mother to daughter. My younger sister, in contrast, seemed to look nothing like us. She looked like our father, inheriting the petite full-busted voluptuous body of his five sisters, along with their minimal derrieres, warm sand-coloured skin, and slightly slanted eyes that seemed to close when she smiled—eyes that harkened back to some precontinental drift Asiatic ancestor. Hers was a more exotic beauty that I envied and wondered why my mother hadn't imparted to me. My sister always longed to look more like our mother and me; she wanted to feel like she belonged to our tribe.

II. Our Mother's Love...

> Love set you going like a fat gold watch.
> The midwife slapped your footsoles, and your bald cry
> Took its place among the elements.
> —Sylvia Plath, "Morning Song" 156

Janice's Voice

Newton's law states that an object will remain in motion unless acted upon by an external force. My mother lived this law of physics, always in motion. We, my sister and I, were the external force, compelling her ceaseless motion and providing the friction that got in her way. She was the mother planet continually revolving around two suns, my sister and myself. We seemed to be the reason for her being. On this swirling axis, she was constantly washing, cooking, cleaning, sweeping, mopping, and sewing—she was always preparing something—while instructing, correcting, and guiding our lives. Perhaps the seeds of this came from my grandmother. From the time she told my grandmother she was pregnant with me, and my grandmother responded that my mother had better not even stub her toe out of fear of miscarriage, my mother's singular purpose in life was the care and covering of my sister and me. She, like the apostle Paul, "poured herself out like a drink offering" for her two daughters, and we greedily sucked up every ounce she had to offer, never fully appreciating the price of that drink. In my earliest memories of my mother, she was a conglomeration of powerful hands, arms, and feet. Once a week, she bent over a bathtub full of clothes with a scrub board, a box of Tide, and a bottle of Clorox bleach; she first washed the white clothes then the coloured ones, all by hand. It would be several years before we could afford a wringer washer that would be hooked up to the kitchen sink. The knuckles on her hands were always red after the hours of rubbing against the board. It was a task that seemed to consume her entire day.

Those hands and arms seemed so strong. In my mind, they were as commanding as Popeye's after eating his spinach. Pumping veins ran up her arms and throughout her hands creating superhuman muscles that powerfully wrung out wet sheets and towels, my father's shirts and pants, our dresses and underwear—all of which would later be placed across radiators and windowsills to dry. We never had a dryer. Later that night, in that same bathtub, those hands would lovingly bathe us, and those arms would tenderly hug us goodnight. She would then go stand on what had to be weary feet over the ironing board until midnight, first starching, then ironing all that she had washed. "Mommy, are you going to bed?" "In a while, baby, I have to iron these clothes while they're still damp." We had no steam iron. My only memory of my mother in repose was when she sat quietly in the living room. As we sat in the kitchen eating the dinner she had prepared, each evening she quietly slipped away into the living room and read the five daily newspapers, the current *Jet* or *Ebony* magazine, her recent selection from the Book-of-the-Month club, or one of the Hollywood scandal sheets. Her books, newspapers, and magazines catapulted her beyond the walls of our four-room apartment, and all of its demands, out into the larger outside world of ideas and discourses. A world in which, on most days, she was in but of which she was not a part.

Mary's Voice
True to her Irish-Catholic heritage, my mother was pregnant eight times over twelve years, bringing to life and nurturing to adulthood seven unique beings who would eventually outgrow her care but never her loving gaze. My mother could have been a juggler in the circus having mastered the art of cradling a baby in one arm and pushing a stroller with two small children crowded inside (this was before double-seated strollers) while instructing another two children to hang tightly onto the sides. There were always diapers soaking in the toilets (this was before disposable diapers), dozens of baby-bottles drying on the dish drain, and heaps of laundry on the landing of the stairs waiting to be tossed to the basement and magically returned as clean, folded clothes for use the next day. As a child, I navigated around these minor obstacles, yelling for a sibling to vacate the diaper-free toilet, climbing over the mountain of laundry, and sometimes kicking and thrashing in the pile for fun or in revenge for the inconvenience it represented to me.

It was only as an adult that these memories came to represent the enormity of the work my mother faced alone each day. As a child, my mother's endless days and nights were invisible to me. She poured herself out to satisfy our thirsty demands; we gulped without any awareness of her sacrifice. Indeed, two of my most vivid childhood memories of my mom were of her fruitless search for some respite from the endless chores she faced each day. Frequently, at least in my memory, upon my return from school, I would find my mother napping on the front-room couch (which she had reupholstered herself), tightly cradling the baby in one arm and trying to get a few moments of shut-eye before we all redescended on the house. In the evening, she hung herself, literally, with a weighted contraption attached to the top of the den door and designed to alleviate the aching, pinched nerve in her neck. As we watched the flickering black-and-white television in the crowded den, sometimes donning the purple floral jackets that she had crafted from the leftover upholstery fabric from the couch, she sat plastered against the den door, her neck stretched and her head and her eyes compelled forwards, trapped in place by forces, which she both chose yet which had also been thrust upon her by circumstances beyond her control.

III. Set Us Spinning…

> We need fully to understand the power and powerlessness embodied in motherhood in patriarchal culture.
> —Adrienne Rich, *Of Woman Born* 67

Mary's Voice

Whereas my mother was the centre of my childhood universe, my father was the sun around which she revolved. It was my father's schedule that dictated the shape of her day, my father's tastes that determined her shopping list, and my father's job that framed the life choices of her marriage and family: where to live, what to eat, and if to vacation. My father loved my mother with an unwavering resilience, which led him to seek her presence whenever possible, to share a television show, to take a short trip to the store, or just to linger over a meal for one minute and talk. My mother, in contrast, sought opportunities to retreat from his dominating presence by burying herself in a book, turning to the dishes waiting in the sink, or playing a card game with one of us kids. My father's love for my mother, though both genuine and deeply private, manifested itself in a culture that demanded her sacrifices for his benefit and then made those benefits invisible to both of them by reducing them to their roles in the family. My father led his family, and his wife, with a stern benevolence that drove his children to academic and professional success and his wife to retreat. I know their relationship did not begin this way. As an adult, I found a diary my mother kept as a teenager. On the pages, I found a frivolous young girl infatuated by the tall, dark, and driven young man that would become my father. My mother chose my father from among many possible options, neighbourhood boys and schoolmates who all, my aunts would later recall, doted on my mother, calling for her attention and companionship. On those pages, she loved my father deeply for himself and not merely for his role in supporting our family. At the beginning of their relationship, she sought my father out, always wanting him nearby, but this I only realized upon reading the pages of that diary.

Janice's Voice

My mother was one of the brightest, funniest, most insightful women I knew and an extraordinary storyteller. I believe my gift for storytelling came from my mother and my grandmother and all those nights my little sister and I sat around the kitchen table listening to them recount stories about their lives growing up in the South and about our various odd relatives. My favourite stories involved my Aunt Jane, a midwife in Alabama who was notorious for the black Stetson hat she wore, the white stallion she rode, and the bullwhip she carried when going to deliver babies. When Aunt Jane became exhausted and frustrated with her husband's beatings, as well as the confiscation of her earnings, she retreated to live in the woods with her horse as her companion. When my mother told these stories, her laughter filled the air, light emanated from her eyes, and power propelled her voice as she shared some perceptive wisdom at the end of her stories. She was transformed into another person, one who was alive and beautiful, one who I aspired to be. Most people who encountered my mother when they came to our home would not know this side of her. She seldom went anywhere unless it was to go shopping for a personal item we needed or something that was needed for the house, to go to the grocery store, or to go to my school for PTA meetings and events when parent volunteers were needed. Her forays into the world beyond our home were always need based. My mother would move mutedly through the spaces of our house, carrying out one task or another while the other women would gather around the kitchen table and talk. She never raised her voice except to reprimand my sister and me for not doing something she had told us to do or for doing something she had told us not to do. She seemed to be in a permanent state of preoccupation and melancholy; when she smiled, it was faint, and when she laughed, it was quiet, not the robust uninhibited laughter that came from the kitchen table.

My father was seldom home. When he was home, he was in the front room watching television—usually a movie or a show about war or a John Wayne western. My parents resided in two separate universes, hers in the back of the house, his in the front. When not watching television, he was sleeping, working the second shift at the post office, or visiting the neighbourhood bar. I watched as my mother's life with my father turned her more and more each day into the "incredible shrinking woman." My mother was a beautiful woman, and he was extremely jealous and didn't want her going anywhere unless he was with her. He was the one who defined the boundaries of her world, and she lived, at least physically, within the borders of those boundaries. I believe, however, that her mind allowed her to often travel beyond those borders. Those books she read as well as the things she knew and talked about when engaging in an uncensored speech at the kitchen table or on the phone with friends or with "Aunt Kitty," our neighbour from upstairs, as they sat playing two-handed whist on Saturday nights—all told me how she often travelled to places and embarked on adventures beyond our home and our limited imaginations of who she was. I don't think there was any malice on my father's part; he, like most men of his generation and society, had very definite ideas about what a good woman was. A good woman stayed at home, kept her house, herself, and her children clean, knew how to cook, took diligent care of her husband, and didn't run the streets. My mother was a good woman:

> "Girls and boys develop different relational capacities and senses of self as a result of growing up in a family in which women mother." Nancy Chodorow, *The Reproduction of Mothering* 173

Mary's Voice

My mom was addicted to several things: cigarettes, card games, and Harlequin romances. I learned to read with Nancy Drew mysteries and devoured the heaving chests, sharp indrawn breaths, and dainty waists of Harlequin romance heroines. My first experience of reading was not as an academic exercise or as a joyful exploration but an escape from whatever homework or responsibility I was avoiding. I surely learned this from my mother. My mother recommended *War and Peace* to all of her children but advised we skim or skip the war chapters, as they were way too dreary. Romance novels were both our escape and our prison. In these novels, our freedom and our choices were manifest in the broad shoulders and brooding desire of someone else, who we could capture but never lead, a hero who would ultimately capture us—the ironic result of the heroine's machinations. My parents' relationship was not a work of fiction, of course, but it echoed those gendered expressions of romantic and familial love. My mother's love for her husband and her children demanded her supporting role in their success and also trapped her in a tangled web of needs and love, obligation, and affection. She ironed shirts for my father and stayed up late, sometimes very late, typing my research papers for school. She packed for his business trips while working on our science projects. Our success was her success. But it was rarely, if ever, the other way around.

In the evening, we girls—my mother and one or more of my sisters—frequently gathered around our big, round kitchen table to play triple (or quadruple) solitaire, rushing to slap our cards in place before our competitors, our sisters, or our mother beat us to it. We laughed and cheerfully argued as my father sat in the den watching the television, occasionally calling for one of us to change the channel (the trials of those pre-remote-control days) or refresh his iced tea. From about the age of ten years old, I, like each of my siblings, knew how to make my father's martini. Using the special, double-sided shot glass that waited at the side of the sink alongside the drying baby bottles, upon his request (or demand), we carelessly sloshed the liquors (two shots of gin from the big side, one shot of vermouth from the small side) into a special gold-trimmed martini glass with a sliver of lemon.

My dad worked long, hard days in a skyscraper in the heart of the city. I had no idea what he did there, something with numbers and prices and a multiple-worded title, but I knew he worked hard. Our life at home, his requests and our responses, including our mother's, recognized those long days that anchored our lives and shaped our futures. Our card playing occupied the space at the margins of that long day outside our home. My mother found joy and companionship around the edges of a life framed by someone else's day, around the edges of a life filled with family responsibilities and arduous, rarely acknowledged, other-directed chores. My mother treasured this life, loved her children dearly and sacrificed willingly for the sake of the family. Indeed, to the extent that a woman can choose her own life given the dictates and unconscious demands of our gendered culture, she chose her life. My aunt, her sister, once recalled how, as a young girl, she longed for babies, many, many babies. I don't believe that my mother ever regretted that choice. But every choice, whether real or a mere illusion, brings loss and regret. This momentous life choice was no different. She never once spoke of this loss. I have no doubt she felt it.

Janice's Voice

My mother smoked Viceroy cigarettes, loved doing crossword puzzles, and was a voracious reader. She usually simultaneously engaged in the act of smoking and reading during the few quiet moments she was able to steal away for herself. These were such private moments that I was always embarrassed to intrude. I often stood quietly in the hallway peeping around the corner watching her read; she was so lovely in my eyes at those times, almost like a still life. She usually sat in profile on the sofa as light softly filtered in from the small window facing the gangway: one arm luxuriously resting on the back of the sofa with a cigarette in hand, legs crossed, book on her lap, gently turning the pages with her other hand. Luckily, I was unconsciously drawn to mirror her reading but not her smoking. I read both Truman Capote's *In Cold Blood* and Harper Lee's *To Kill a Mockingbird* as an eleven-year-old. Every month, I anxiously waited for her Book-of-the-Month Club selection. As we got closer to the middle of the month when the book came, I would often ask her, "Is it time for the book yet?" She would smile and say, "Not yet but soon." I think my enthusiasm pleased her. After she read each month's selection, she would place it in the small bookcase built into the headboard of her bed along with her other books. She would say, "The book is in the headboard." I would then climb up on her bed, retrieve the book, and return it after I finished reading it. We never had discussions about the books, whether I enjoyed them or even if I understood what I was reading. It was the act of reading that we quietly shared.

When my sister and I came home each day from school and if we didn't have homework, we had to read for an hour. When we came home and even if we did have homework, after we finished, we had to read for an hour. When we were small, my mother would walk us to our neighbourhood library every two weeks to take out books. It was during those times that she would talk about reading, sharing with us some of the stories she had read, building our anticipation of what was waiting for us in the library. Once we were older, every other Friday we were expected to go on our own to the library and sign out books. During those times, I missed my mother's presence and the stories she shared as we walked. The trips to the library were never the same.

IV. Round and Round…

> I loved you even during the years
> When you knew nothing
> And I knew everything, I loved you still.
> Condescendingly of course,
> From my high perch
> Of teenage wisdom.
> —Maya Angelou, *Mother, A Cradle to Hold Me* 25

Janice's Voice

I don't know when I started seeing my mother's quiet gentleness as a weakness. Her seemingly total submission to my father's will was something that I never understood or wanted for my life if I ever got married. I, in no way, wanted to be like her. Somewhere along the way, I lost perspective on those strong arms that could tirelessly wring out wet sheets and towels as well as the intelligent woman who read all five of the city's daily newspapers every single day and a new novel every two weeks. I started to judge her and the life she led. In the late 1960s, times were changing, the world was loud, and women were roaring and not whispering. They were using their outside voices inside and demanding to be heard. What it meant to be a strong woman looked nothing like what I saw in my mother. She seemed overwhelmingly passive and inadequate in my eyes. I didn't see her as a fighter and was ashamed of her, and she knew it. One day in a fit of adolescent rage, I shouted this loudly to her: "The only reason I respect you is that you are my mother, and I have to, and that's all!" She looked at me with eyes filled with hurt and simply said, "Janice Faye, just go to your room." Even though I knew I broke her heart that day, she remained consistently herself. The idea of that moment continues to shame me and break my heart, and I spent most of my adult life making amends for it.

The problem was I was looking at my mother through the wrong lens. While I was busy comparing my mother to those who I thought were the more powerful progressive women in the country, I didn't see how she was launching her own feminist campaign in her own small world. When I was in seventh grade, my mother and grandmother went downtown shopping one day. My mother came back home with a job. After lunch and a slow gin fizz for courage, she had walked over to Goldblatt's Department Store on State Street, applied for a job, and succeeded. After that, a cold polite silence filled our house. My father walked around the house for two weeks not speaking to my mother, angry that she had gotten a job. "What will people think about me if you start working? They will think I can't support my family!" he shouted. He tried to force her to quit. She refused. It was the beginning of the end of their relationship. My mother started as a stock girl and worked her way up to a salesperson in the ladies' shoe department. She was the first woman to sell ladies' shoes on State Street at a time when only men sold women their shoes. I didn't recognize the significance of her accomplishment until much later. All I noticed was the void that was left in the house once she started working and the chores I had to learn as a result. I later learned my mother had worked since she was sixteen years old and only quit working when she married and had children. She had always planned to resume working outside the home once my sister and I were out of elementary school. In my tunnel vision, I only saw this woman as my mother and not the quiet calculating revolutionary who was biding her time.

Mary's Voice

My mother's gentleness infuriated me. Why couldn't she just post a list of chores and enforce the list? Why? Her preferred leadership style with her children revolved around catching whichever child was closest to press them into action. Please take the garbage out. Please change the batch of laundry down the basement. Please fetch the bleach so I can finish scouring the tub. Please peel these potatoes. Each request was met with an endless barrage of excuses and refusals. Why me? Maybe later, not now! Not possible, on my way out. Too much homework. Bad stomach ache. This isn't fair. Definitely, not fair. More frequently than not, the captured child escaped, and my mother toiled on alone, regretting the time wasted with the entreaties. In reflecting on my aunt's more dictatorial style of mothering, my mom once observed that either way, the process is exhausting: The enforcement is as endless as the chores themselves.

I concluded silently that when I became a mother, I would choose the enforcement of a posted set of clear chores over actually doing the chores myself. Until I had children of my own that is. Then, faced with the unbridled determination of an eight-year-old, I wavered. It was not only the exhaustion that caused me to waver but also that my relationship with that child was framed by a history of endless giving and thoughtless, gulping receiving—a giving and receiving founded both in biological necessity (the infant's immense need and vulnerability) and also my love for that greedy little creature. It became difficult to distinguish my ends, goals, and desires. My child's ends became my ends, my child's happiness inseparable from my own. Once I had been the recipient of that endless love, basking in that love and gulping down the care of my mother. Now, as the giver, as the mother, I understood how one could lose oneself in that bottomless well of love and need.

V. Grounding Our Turns, Setting Us Free

> And so because you love me, and because
> I love you, Mother, I have woven a wreath
> Of rhymes wherewith to crown your honoured name:
> In you not fourscore years can dim the flame
> Of love, whose blessed glow transcends the laws
> Of time and change and mortal life and death.
>
> —Rossetti, "Sonnets Are Full of Love"

Mary's Voice

My mother taught me so many things. She taught me how to play cards with wild abandon, pushing others aside to slap cards into place with a light-hearted determination to win. She taught me to read for the sheer pleasure of reading, momentarily putting aside urgent tasks and heart-pounding anxieties. She taught me how to make huge pots of food, stews, chilies, soups—all of which were remarkably similar in taste and prepared to nourish the hearts and bodies of those she loved. She taught me how to comfort a crying baby, swaddling the writhing, screaming infant close to my breast, mending our bodies seamlessly back together, shifting hips and feet, and rhythmically erasing the flow of time that had separated us.

This last skill was not so much learned as acquired—a way of life that demanded that one approach each task while also attending to the needs of another person who is both of, and not of, oneself. My mother taught me how to firmly grasp that screaming infant, thrust a pacifier into its cavernous mouth, and firmly press that mouth to my breast, compelling the child to suck, calming both the baby's cries and my aching heart. With years of practice, my mother could comfort a baby while tending to a variety of other tasks, washing greasy dishes, combing a wiggly toddler's knotty hair, or lugging a batch of laundry up the stairs. In a moment of respite, she would cradle an infant in one arm, which also held a book open, while also smoking a Virginia Slims cigarette and monitoring the variety of children swarming around her.

Janice's Voice

The woman and mother I am today are because of my mother. It was through the life I saw her live, the wisdom she shared, and her ability for quiet restraint in situations where I would have wanted to scream—not that she didn't also scream at us on occasion—that I learned to mother. I marvel at all she and so many other women of her generation were able to accomplish with so few of the modern conveniences of today, all while trying to find some way to sustain their dreams and desires for personal growth. I fell in love with my mother all over again once I had children of my own. I came to understand my mother so much more clearly. She was my refuge and sensei to whom I ran when the treacherous waters of motherhood felt like they were going to take me under.

As adults, we established a weekly meeting that I called Blue Mondays. Every Monday, my sister would pick me up from my job when she got off from work. We would then stop by the store, pick up a bottle of wine, and head to our mother's house. There the three of us sat at her kitchen table sipping wine with our mother's jazz albums softly playing in the background—Billie Holiday, Sarah Vaughan, Dinah Washington, all the sad girl singers, hence the name Blue Mondays. Our mother would allow us to ask her questions about life, and she would answer as best she could. I once asked my mother, "How did you keep all the balls in the air that went along with being a mother without dropping them?" She smiled and simply said, "You just do what you have to do. Sometimes you do drop a ball. You have to forgive yourself and hope that things will turn out alright." She then laughed and said, "In the case of you and your sister, everything did for the most part." Agreeing with her, I took a deep gulp from my wine glass. With mothering, we all must find our own way to drink from the cup we are given. On another occasion when I was on my second glass of wine, with tears in my eyes, I asked her, "Why didn't you tell me? Why didn't you tell me how hard it was?" She looked at me with a small smile and tears in her own eyes, more for me than for herself, and said, "Because you wouldn't have believed me if I had." I nodded, knowing she was right. Beyond the biological stages of pregnancy, no one can prepare you ahead of time for this thing called mothering. It is one of those jobs you learn to do while doing it. I raised my glass to my mother and took another sip of wine, thankful that I had her beside me to help guide my way.

VI. Janice and Mary in One Voice

> From the start
> our mother's love
> set us spinning
> round and round
> grounding our turns, setting us free.
>
> —Janice Tuck Lively and Mary Barbara Walsh

More than forty years ago, Adrienne Rich called for the recognition of a distinction between the institution of mothering and the potential of mothering. Through an examination of history, philosophy, and feminism, and with insights gained through her relationships with her mother and children, Rich pointed to the difference between the institution of mothering, which is inextricably bound to the patriarchal forces in which it is actualized, and the potential of mothering, which is tied to the essentially human, everyday—mundane and profound—labour of mothering. The reciprocal narratives articulated here, like the narratives of every other mother and child, illustrate both the pain of mothering and the possibility of joy rooted in the potential of mothering—a joy resonant in the profound connection between mother and child. Mothering, as it is tied to the exhausting work and exhilarating labour of relationships founded in care and need, is also tied to the infinite love and binding obligations persons realize in caring for one another.

Each of the narratives articulated here illustrates not only the particularities of a mother's love as it is actualized in a racist, classist, and patriarchal society but also the potential of mothering for grounding deep, genuine love. But our voices are merely two among many voices—an infinite number of voices across the globe and through history, voices as varied as the time and the geography in which they emerged. Disentangling the pervasive, patriarchal aspects of historically realized mothering from the potential of mothering demands that we listen to and engage with the infinite ways in which mothering is actualized. Perhaps, discourse founded in friendship, whether across a boardroom or a sandbox, an international border or a cultural divide, spoken or written, provides an avenue to disentangling those historically contingent aspects of mothering from the essential character of mothering. And, in this way, in friendship and a spirit of a growing community, we can continue to challenge the gender oppression endemic in historical, patriarchal mothering while recognizing the joy and fundamental humanity of mothering.

Works Cited

Angelou, Maya. *Mother, A Cradle to Hold Me.* Random House, 2006.

Chodorow, Nancy. *The Reproduction of Mothering.* University of California Press, 1978.

Lugones, Maria, and Elizabeth Spelman. 'Have we Got a Theory for You! Feminist Theory, Cultural Imperialism and the Demand for "The Woman's Voice"' *Feminist Philosophies,* 2nd ed., edited by Janet Kourany, James Sterba and Rosemarie Tong, Prentice Hall, 1999, pp. 474-86.

Plath, Sylvia. "Morning Song." *The Poetry Foundation,* www.poetry foundation.org/poems/49008/morning-song-56d22ab4a0cee Accessed 19 Feb. 2022.

Rich, Adrienne. *Of Woman Born: Motherhood as Experience and Institution.* W.W. Norton & Company, 1976.

Rossetti, Christina. *Poems.* Macmillan and Co., 1890.

Sale, Maggie. "Call and Response as Critical Method: African-American Oral Traditions and *Beloved.*" *African American Review,* vol 26, no. 1, 1992, pp. 41-50.

Yin, Steph. "Why Do We Inherit Mitochondrial DNA Only From Our Mothers?" *The New York Times,* 23 June 2016, www.nytimes.com/2016/06/24/science/mitochondrial-dna-mothers.html. Accessed 19 Feb. 2022.

Chapter 13

A "Community of Comothers": How Friendships with Expatriate Mothers Create Intercultural Understanding

Meredith Stephens

> Many mothers ... feel part of a community of comothers whose warmth and support is rarely equalled in other working relationships.
>
> —Sara Ruddick 343

As an Australian expatriate mother in Japan, I formed friendships not only with Japanese mothers but also with Chinese, British, Kenyan, American, Canadian, Argentinian, Filipina, and Russian mothers. The experience of raising children in a foreign country created a bond with these mothers that transcended cultural differences. This connects to Lynn O'Brien Hallstein's experiences as an expatriate mother in Switzerland when she explains how her expatriate friendships were a source of sustenance and cultural diversity. Similarly, Erika de Jong Watanabe, an expatriate mother in Japan, expresses her gratitude to the community of foreign women and their children that she belonged to. This chapter explores my friendships with other mothers that may not have been created so quickly if we had been in our own countries with our extended family support systems. Now that our children have grown, many of us remain firm friends, despite the original reason for our friendship no longer being so compelling.

My entry into motherhood coincided with the time when my spouse found a teaching contract in Japan. He relocated before me, and I followed him once the doctor had given me the all clear to travel when my daughter Eloise was eight weeks old. This happened at one of the most vulnerable times in my life—the timing of the birth of my first child coincided with separation from friends and family.

Once I arrived in Japan with Eloise, the first friendships I formed were with Japanese mothers in the neighbourhood. They helped me navigate the Japanese medical system, took me shopping, and taught me to make Japanese baby food by boiling rice until it turned into a thick soup known as *okayu*. They taught me things such as how to make Japanese dishes, such as fried rice and Japanese-style pizza. They were very thoughtful, buying baby clothes for Eloise or leaving freshly baked bread at my door. They shared their language with me and in so doing invited me to use the Japanese language skills I had worked so hard over many years at school and university to achieve. More than two decades later—well after our children have grown—they continue to share their precious, endlessly challenging language with me.

These Japanese mothers helped me adjust to life in Japan, but there were other mothers—expatriate mothers—who also served an important role in my adjustment. The expatriate mothers enhanced my ability to adapt to the demands of childrearing in Japan because of our shared position as outsiders. Unlike Japanese mothers, most expatriate mothers have been uprooted from the usual support of mothers, sisters, and those of their partners. Expatriate mothers in Japan must navigate health and education systems in Japanese, and the accompanying language shift entails a cultural shift. A new language embodies different values and assumptions, cross-cultural differences that must be negotiated by expatriate mothers from all backgrounds. Accordingly, expatriate mothers tend to educate each other about the health and education systems, and these shared concerns of mothers override cultural differences. As Rachel Epp Buller states, "I idealistically believe that any two mothers might find some common experience through which to discourse" (186), and as Sara Ruddick argues, compellingly, "Many mothers, whatever their work in the public world, feel part of a community of comothers whose warmth and support is rarely equalled in other working relationships" (344).

In this discussion, "community" refers to a group of people with shared interests and goals, who meet in person to offer and receive support. Sherry Turkle explains that the literal meaning of community is "to give among each other" (238). She stresses the real-life nature of community as opposed to the virtual world: "Communities are constituted by physical proximity, shared concerns, real consequences, and common responsibilities. Its members help each other in the most practical ways" (239). Similarly, Susan Pinker stresses the importance of physical proximity in building relationships, elucidating the power of face-to-face social contact in real-time in her exposition of *The Village Effect*. She argues that social bonds are just as transformative as breakthroughs in diet, exercise, and pharmaceutical drugs, highlighting the power of close contact with others, particularly with women.

Belonging to such a community may even transcend cultural belonging because the needs of the present are so compelling. The reality of caring for children in the present time and space in the host culture is a powerful force in the formation of a community. One such learning community in Japan is an English-language circle for English-speaking children attending public Japanese preschools and elementary schools, which has evolved into a cooperative learning circle (Thompson). Parents took turns teaching their subject areas to the children in the community. An expatriate community of comothers in Japan also appeared in Suzanne Kamata's fiction. One of her short stories ("Polishing the Halo") featured a group of expatriate comothers who met at the Foreign Wives Club and who offered the protagonist support when she disclosed to them that her young daughter was deaf.

First, I will describe four of my expatriate mother friends from Canada, China, the United States, and Kenya and explain how they helped me understand not only Japanese culture but also their cultures. Second, I will discuss how my expatriate friends helped me make decisions about how to either conform to local expectations of mothers and mothering or to maintain aspects of the many and varied Western models of mothering. Three of the four mothers in this discussion are academics, and the fourth is the spouse of an academic.

How the Friendships Formed

Marie-Christine. One of my first friendships with another expatriate mother was with Marie-Christine, a Québécoise married to Taro and mother to their son, Tomo. Marie-Christine and I were the only full-time Western women on the university campus and shared the unusual features of brown hair, pale skin, and pale eyes. It is unlikely that we would be mistaken for each other in a Western country, but in Japan, these shared features were different enough from the rest of the population that some local people could not distinguish between us. Once I was publicly upbraided by a member of the clerical staff for not filling in a form correctly, and I confronted her for mistaking me for Marie-Christine. (I later regretted not having had the discretion and quick thinking to assume Marie-Christine's identity and apologise for the presumed error.) Our children attended different schools and did not have the opportunity to play together, but Marie-Christine and I often shared the tribulations of navigating our children's high school entrance exams as well as being the only Western parents of children in our children's respective schools.

As foreign mothers, we were unable to conform to all of the demands made on us by the schools (see also Kamata, "An Introduction"; Ogasahara; Jones-Nakanishi; Stigger). We could privately commiserate at the consequences of our intercultural incompetence, although I must stress that Marie-Christine in no way conformed to my slapdash approach to food preparation for children's obento lunches (see Stephens). There were many ways in which both of us struggled to conform to unfamiliar expectations. I find some comfort, if not justification, for this in Nel Noddings' explanation of the role of caring: "The commitment to caring invokes a duty to promote skepticism and noninstitutional affiliation" (103). We looked out for our children's interests in ways that cannot be expected of an institution, such as a school. Japanese schools may have as many as forty in a class, and like any other institution, there is a myriad of rules and regulations. As outsiders, there were unfamiliar rules (such as strict rules forbidding hair dyeing), and when we were perplexed as to how to support our children in conforming to these rules, we could consult each other.

Nearly twenty years later, our children have left home and now attend university, but we still maintain our friendship from each end of the island and exchange photographs and updates of our dogs on social media. Our professional relationship has also thrived, and recently we presented together at an international congress on second language reading in Tokyo. We have been able to support each other as friends and professionals over the twenty years, and this friendship sprung from a shared position of being Western mothers of bilingual toddlers in rural Japan.

Zhi-Zhi. Once I had mastered the intricacies of daily life in Japan, I was able to help other foreign newcomers. The first mother I was able to help was a Chinese scholar at the university, who had come to Japan to research classical Chinese documents housed in Japanese libraries. My daughters were several years older than her toddler. I knew where the childcare centres were and had insider information, such as the fact that mothers have to provide futons for their child's daily nap. I did the rounds of the daycare centres with Zhi-Zhi but because of our ethnic appearances, the staff at each daycare centre thought that she was the local and I was the foreigner. Contrary to appearances, I was the Japanese speaker, and it took a while for the staff to realize that I was interpreting for her, not vice versa. This comic routine helped forge our friendship. I was later able to pass on to her baby goods that my children had grown out of. In turn, she invited my daughters and me to the best Chinese restaurant in town, staffed by resident Chinese. I was able to learn more about her research area than otherwise because of the time we spent together, resulting from the bond created by motherhood. I had made my first friend from mainland China, forged through our shared experience of expatriate mothering.

Suzanne. My hometown Adelaide, in the south of Australia, is geographically isolated, not only within Australia but also globally. An unanticipated bonus of relocating to Japan was the opportunity to make connections with expatriates from distant regions of the anglosphere. One of these friendships was with the US writer Suzanne Kamata, whose reputation had preceded her. I was delighted to learn about her from another Australian expatriate mother, who told me that a prize-winning author of fiction was living in the same city on our small island Shikoku. When I first met Suzanne, she had just published her first novel, *Losing Kei*, and over the years, I witnessed her publish a succession of novels, including *Gadget Girl, Screaming Divas, The Mermaids of Lake Michigan, Indigo Girl,* and the travel memoir *A Girls'*

Guide to the Islands. The pivotal moment for me was when I was invited to her creative writing workshop. Until meeting her, my writing had been confined to second language pedagogy, childhood bilingualism, and comparative education. Suzanne introduced me to the topic of expatriate motherhood, and this provided me with a channel to reflect upon and to express my experience of spending many years as a mother living on Shikoku. Not only that, but Suzanne also has an intense commitment to writing. None of my other friends or acquaintances had expressed a passion like this, and after observing Suzanne, I permitted myself to commit to writing. Suzanne had edited an anthology about expatriate motherhood, for which she provides the following rationale in her introduction: "Instead of thinking back to my own childhood or looking to the Japanese mothers around me for guidelines, I often feel the urge to consult with other mothers raising their children across cultures. Thus, this book was born" ("Introduction" 4). Suzanne's anthology provides stories of expatriate mothers around the globe. Although I was unable to cast as widely as Suzanne in search of global voices, I was able to connect with expatriate mothers from around the globe on our small island.

Imogen. When my younger daughter Annika started middle school, I assumed that she would be the only foreign student. I was surprised and delighted to learn that there was a girl from Kenya in her class. The common experience of being foreigners was the impetus for them to reach out to each other, and they soon became best friends. Annika was English-Japanese bilingual whereas her Kenyan friend, Louise, was multilingual: Louise was proficient in English and Japanese and understood both Kikuyu and Swahili. Annika and Louise were both speakers of English and Japanese, and both of them had two foreign parents. Louise's Japanese was so advanced that she would converse with her Kenyan mother, Imogen, in Japanese. Imogen's Japanese was also impeccable, and she was accepted as a Japanese speaker in the local community. After Annika and Louise became friends, I developed a friendship with Imogen. Imogen was more than ten years younger than me and came from a distant culture, but the shared experience of being foreign mothers on the island of Shikoku enabled us to forge a bond. Imogen and her partner were the first expatriates from an African nation in our city, but others were to follow. They formed friendships with members of the African diaspora, and I found myself in the happy position of being invited to African parties in Japan. I learned firsthand about their views on colonization and its legacy, about their many languages and cultures.

Our views on education differed. Imogen adhered closely to local norms in her mothering, so Louise had a strict study routine to enable her to succeed in the competitive round of examinations to enter a well-regarded high school. Because of her proficient Japanese, Imogen was more in tune with the views of Japanese mothers, and the value she placed on disciplined preparation paid off when Louise gained entry to a prestigious high school. I remained a skeptic, not to say a rebel, regarding the correlation between hours of study and academic success, and so I sent Annika to tennis lessons after school rather than cram school. As could be predicted from our parenting strategies, our daughters' educational outcomes differed. Louise maintained her work ethic throughout high school and earned a scholarship to a university in Tokyo. In contrast, my attitude towards homework did not equip Annika for success in the Japanese educational system, and she transferred to the Australian system in Year Eleven. Louise is at university in Tokyo, and Annika at university in Australia, but Imogen and I have maintained our friendship. The shared experience of expatriate motherhood in rural Japan was the impetus for friendship and cultural exchange with someone of different age and from a distant culture.

How the Community of Comothers Creates Intercultural Understanding

Epp Buller discusses the resentment many mothers feel at being judged: "Mothering is such a highly charged relational context, where one can feel judged over private decisions about breastfeeding, diapering, childcare, discipline, sleeping arrangements, and so on" (186). I will now explain how my expatriate friends helped me make my own decisions about issues such as these, particularly when I chose to conform to Japanese cultural expectations and reject my own, and vice versa. Each of the private decisions mentioned by Epp Buller varies cross-culturally and also within cultures. My friends in the community of comothers demonstrated how they balanced the expectations of the society with those of their own culture. As a result, I am in the unusual position of having raised children according to Western customs in some aspects and Japanese tradition in others. My interactions with expatriate comothers informed my choices about breastfeeding, sleeping arrangements, education, cultural capital (fostering the language of the home), extracurricular activities, public bathing, and making local Japanese friends.

Breastfeeding. One area in which cultural differences emerged was the choice of whether to supplement breastmilk with formula as well as the timing of weaning a baby. Having had my babies in Australia, I was urged to exclusively breastfeed. Upon arrival in Japan, I was told my baby was underweight and was urged to supplement her diet with formula. This was before the days of the ease of electronic communications, and I had no support from my mother or sisters or those of my spouse. After the birth of Annika, I was relieved to make an expatriate friend whose baby was three months younger than mine. My friend confidently breastfed her baby well beyond the years when Japanese mothers breastfed theirs, and her confidence in this decision inspired me to breastfeed Annika if she wanted to.

Sleeping arrangements. My Japanese friends slept alongside their babies and other children, and their partners slept alone in another room. When I returned on visits to Australia, health professionals urged against cosleeping. The method of helping babies to sleep away from their mothers was called "controlled crying," in which the mother would allow the baby to cry in her room for progressively longer periods before going in her room to comfort her. Allowing my baby to cry and refraining from comforting her went against my instincts, but the health professionals in Australia, and my spouse's mother, were insistent that I persist with this. They reassured me that eventually my baby would give up crying and learn to sleep on her own. However, she refused to do this, and it was unbearable to listen to her pleas for comfort. The Japanese habit of having the baby sleep alongside the mother in her baby futon felt instinctively right. Meanwhile, in Japan, an expatriate comother had adopted the Japanese habit of having her baby sleep in her room while her partner slept in a separate room. In the end, I found a compromise and spent the next ten years sleeping in the parents' room and moving over to the children's room whenever I heard a cry. I used to boast to my friends at my martyrdom at not having had unbroken sleep for ten years. Perhaps my partner's mother had been right.

Education. The first educational choice concerned kindergarten. My expatriate friends and I would spend hours debating the merits and demerits of each kindergarten. Kindergarten is spread over three years in Japan, between ages three and six. The many private kindergartens are based on varying educational philosophies. One kindergarten was Montessori based, in which classes consist of mixed age groups. Children wore a navy-blue serge uniform, and mothers had to provide a smock. Another kindergarten stressed the value of free play in natural surroundings, and children were allowed to soil their clothes. Without the discussion in English with my expatriate friends, I would have been ill equipped to make an informed choice or to critically consider the philosophical underpinnings of each kindergarten.

The next choice to be deliberated was to find a primary school. As our children were visibly identified as being different and as we were living on a sparsely populated island, they would attract attention from others. The size of the school was important; in a large school, there would be more people looking at them and making comments about them. An expatriate friend considered that a small primary school would be best because the smaller community would acclimatize themselves to our foreign children and perhaps forget their foreignness. Upon relocation to a city at the other end of Shikoku, I followed my expatriate friend's advice and enrolled my child in the smallest school within walking distance. This decision proved to be astute. Annika was tall for her age, and fair, and her appearance was so different from the Japanese children that I could easily identify her from a distance. The school was in the inner city, in a town in which the centre had been hollowed out: Younger families had built houses in the suburbs, known as "the doughnut phenomenon." The inner-city school was so small that there was only one class for each grade, consisting of only about twenty students each. My expatriate friend's advice proved to be right. The Japanese children quickly became friends with my daughter and, I believe, came to see past her foreignness.

Cultural capital. Anna Kurokcycka-Shultz refers to Bourdieu's notion of cultural capital to explain how mothers transmit skills to their children in the interests of upward mobility. She identifies the home language as a form of cultural capital that mothers can confer on their children by interacting with them exclusively in that language. I shared the desire to foster the home language and culture with expatriate comothers. This shared value served to strengthen our friendship as we compared our choice of the languages we used to address our children.

Extracurricular activities. Another form of cultural capital involved our choices of extracurricular activities for our children. Japanese mothering shares many of the features described by Linda Rose Ennis *(Intensive Mothering)*, such as putting the children's needs before the mother's and doing the children's laundry and lunches. The exception is chauffeuring children because Japanese children tend to walk or cycle to school and extracurricular activities by themselves. The mother does bear responsibility for her children's educational outcomes. As Ennis explains: "One of the best ways to be an intensive mother is by introducing and involving one's child in many extra-curricular activities, even if one can't afford to do so or even if one is physically and emotionally drained" ("Epilogue" 334). In Japan, many primary-school children attend supplementary classes in academic subjects, such as maths, Japanese, and English as well as traditional subjects, such as calligraphy and abacus. Many learn the piano or violin, sports such as swimming, basketball, and tennis, and ballet. O'Brien Hallstein rightly observes that "The intensive ideology works to regulate women by demanding impossible-for-most-women-to-meet standards of mothering" (107). I compared myself to Japanese mothers, who prioritized enrolling their children in supplementary education in academic subjects. Although I worried about my children falling behind in maths and Japanese, I could not bring myself to have them continue to study academic subjects at the end of the long school day. As a Westerner, the importance of rest and the temporal boundaries between work and play were too deeply ingrained for me to subscribe to local norms. I considered that participating in extra classes of maths and Japanese after school may even be counterproductive. Maybe too much time devoted to academic study would result in resistance and apathy.

One expatriate friend enrolled her daughter in none of these supplementary classes, and I drew inspiration from her to resist following the norm. However, another expatriate friend subscribed to local norms and had her daughter attend supplementary classes and would not let her play during the time allocated for homework. As I witnessed these varying attitudes, I was able to make my own decision according to my values. Although not much of a sportswoman or dancer myself, I performed my type of peculiar intensive mothering by enrolling Eloise and Annika in physical activities such as swimming, ballet, tennis, volleyball, and basketball. In my idealism, I considered the study to be pursued because of its intrinsic interest, not because of the need to compete with others in entrance examinations. The model provided by another expatriate mother gave me the confidence to affirm my choice.

Public bathing. It took me ten years to develop the courage to enter a spa, known as an *onsen* in Japanese. A British mother would regularly invite me to join her family in the weekly bathing ritual, but I was too embarrassed to countenance it, and instead, my daughters would join her family. She kept entreating me to join her, suggesting it would be the perfect way to help me relax. Finally, years after hearing about the pleasures of the onsen, I ventured in. My initial fears were allayed; none of the other bathers gave me the slightest attention. I was able to regularly enjoy carbonated baths, aloe baths, walking baths, outdoor baths, muddy baths, baths to lie down in and watch television from, pulsating electric baths, jet baths, tub baths for a sole person, and cold baths, for years to come. My British friend and I could never overcome our cultural inhibitions to enter the public bath at the same time, but after observing our daughters adapt to and enjoy this cultural practice, I bravely decided to embrace it in the company of my daughters and eventually other comothers.

Making Japanese friends. My expatriate friends each had their circles of Japanese friends, and our friendship circles widened when we met our friends' friends at social gatherings. It can be difficult for a sole Westerner to make Japanese friends when their child attends kindergarten. Erika de Jong explains that the first friends she made in Japan were not other mothers at the kindergarten but rather other foreign women outside of this circle. She states that she does not have any Japanese friends and feels alone at school events, as Japanese mothers will not talk to her. I was saved from this aloneness, at least some of the time, by a British friend introducing me to Japanese mothers at my daughter's kindergarten. This provided an entrée into a circle of Japanese mothers at the kindergarten, and we could regularly visit one another's houses, climb to the summit of the castle on the mountain together, go out dancing, and go out for lunch or dinner. Annika had more Japanese playmates, and I could leave her at these friends' houses when I was busy.

Conclusions

Some friendships with expatriate comothers were forged because of our daughters' friendships. Others were forged because of the shared experience of being mothers of children in an unfamiliar educational system. These friendships not only were a source of pleasure and solace but also enhanced my understanding of how to be a mother. I was placed in a culture of intensive mothering that was different from the Western model of intensive mothering. The friendships with expatriate comothers provided a counterweight to the model provided by both my own culture and Japanese norms. They gave me the freedom, confidence, and empowerment to make my own choices regarding childrearing.

Since our children have become independent, we maintain our friendships from a considerable distance, comparing notes on our empty nests and children's universities. There was a shared core of the experience of motherhood that transcended our cultural differences, and beyond this core, there were indeed cultural differences. Besides making close friends and becoming an empowered mother, I also developed an understanding of the lived experience, history, geography, and education systems of both near and distant cultures.

Note: Pseudonyms have been used for family and friends, other than the writer Suzanne Kamata.

Works Cited

Ennis, Linda Rose. "Intensive Mothering: Revisiting the Issue Today." *Intensive Mothering: The Cultural Contradictions of Modern Motherhood*, edited by Linda Rose Ennis, Demeter Press, 2014, pp. 1-23.

Ennis, Linda Rose. "Epilogue: Balancing Separation-Connection in Mothering." *Intensive Mothering: The Cultural Contradictions of Modern Motherhood*, edited by Linda Rose Ennis, Demeter Press, 2014, pp. 332-37.

Epp Buller, Rachel. "Representing Motherhood: Reading the Maternal

Body in Contemporary Art." *Mothering in the Third Wave*, edited by Amber E. Kinser, Demeter Press, 2008, pp. 186-97.

Jones-Nakanishi, Wendy. "Mothering Sons in Japan." *Mothering in the Third Wave*, edited by Amber E. Kinser, Demeter Press, 2008, pp. 126-35.

Jong Watanabe, Erika de. "A Parent's Perspective on Raising Bilingual/Bicultural Children: A First Person Account." *Raising Bilingual and Bicultural Children in Japan: Essays from the inaka. Monographs on Bilingualism*, edited by Darren Lingley and Paul Daniels, *JALT Bilingualism SIG*, no. 18, 2018, pp. 115-30.

Kamata, Suzanne. "An Introduction." *Call me Okaasan: Adventures in Multicultural Mothering*, edited by Suzanne Kamata, Wyatt-MacKenzie Publishing, 2009, pp. 7-13.

Kamata, Suzanne. "Polishing the Halo." *The Beautiful One has Come*. Wyatt-MacKenzie Publishing, 2011.

Kurokcycka Shultes, Anna. "Foreign Mothers, Native Children: The Impact of Language on Cultural Identity among Polish Americans in Chicago." *The Migrant Maternal: "Birthing" New Lives Abroad*, edited by Anna Kurokcycka Shultes and Helen Vallianatos, Demeter Press, 2016, pp. 174-89.

Noddings, Nel. *Caring: A Relational Approach to Ethics and Moral Education*. University of California Press, 2013.

O'Brien Hallstein, D. Lynn. "Second Wave Silences and Third Wave Intensive Mothering." *Mothering in the Third Wave*, edited by Amber E. Kinser, Demeter Press, 2008, pp. 107-18.

Ogasawara, Maiko. "A Tale of Three Minority Mums." *Raising Bilingual and Bicultural Children in Japan: Essays from the Inaka. Monographs on Bilingualism*, No. 18, edited by Darren Lingley and Paul Daniels, *JALT Bilingualism SIG*, 2018, pp. 157-68.

Pinker, Susan. *The Village Effect: Why Face-to-face Contact Matters*. Atlantic Books, 2014.

Ruddick, Sara. "Maternal Thinking." *Feminist Studies*, vol. 6, no. 2, 1980, pp. 342-67.

Stephens, Meredith. "The Rebellious Bento Box: Slapdash Western Mothering in Perfectionist Japan." *What's Cooking, Mom? Narratives about Food and Family*, edited by Tanya Cassidy and Florence Pasche-

Guignard, Demeter Press, 2015, pp. 227-42.

Stigger, Elizabeth. "Challenging the Values of being Bilingual." *Raising Bilingual and Bicultural Children in Japan: Essays from the Inaka. Monographs on Bilingualism*, No. 18, edited by Darren Lingley and Paul Daniels, *JALT Bilingualism SIG*, 2018, pp. 37-50.

Thompson, Holly. "Two Versions of Immersion." *Call Me Okaasan: Adventures in Multicultural Mothering*, edited by Suzanne Kamata, Wyatt-MacKenzie Publishing, 2009, pp. 113-23.

Turkle, Sherry. *Alone Together: Why We Expect More from Technology and Less from Each Other.* Basic Books, 2011.

Notes on Contributors

Angela Castañeda, PhD, is a professor of anthropology at DePauw University. Her research in Brazil, Colombia, Mexico, and the US explores questions on religion, ritual, expressive culture, as well as the cultural politics of reproduction, birth, and motherhood. Her current projects focus on the role of doulas in birth culture. Dr. Castañeda is co-editor of *Doulas and Intimate Labour* (Demeter Press, 2015) and *Obstetric Violence* (Demeter Press, 2022).

Skye Chernichky-Karcher, PhD, is an assistant professor in the Department of Communication Studies at Bloomsburg University. She and her spouse welcomed their first child in November 2017.

Rachel D. Davidson, PhD, is an assistant professor at Hanover College, in the Department of Communication. She has an MA from Indiana University Purdue University Indianapolis, in applied communication and a PhD from the University of Wisconsin-Milwaukee in rhetorical/public communication, with certificates in rhetorical leadership and women's studies. Rachel began her career at Hanover College in 2015. Since 2017, she has served as co-coordinator for Hanover College's Speaking Across the Disciplines Program. Her research broadly addresses rhetoric and public culture with interests in motherhood, caregiving, and social advocacy. Rachel's research has appeared in *Communication Quarterly*, *Women and Language*, *Rhetoric of Health and Medicine*, *Disability Studies Quarterly*, and *Gender, Education, Music, and Society (GEMS)*. She has also contributed chapters to academic books on motherhood and popular culture. In 2020, Rachel was the recipient of Hanover College's Daryl R. Karns Award for Scholarly and Creative Activity.

Essah Díaz is a doctoral student of literature and languages of the Caribbean in English at the University of Puerto Rico, Rio Piedras campus. Her poems and essays have been published in print and online publications, including *Moko Magazine, Eclectica Magazine, Tonguas, Odradek*, and *The Odyssey Online* and *Creative Contradictions*. She has coedited a collection of essays from the Caribbean Without Borders March 2020 Conference to be published by the University of Curaçao.

Catherine A. Dobris, PhD, is an Associate Professor at Indiana University Purdue University Indianapolis, in the Department of Communication Studies. She holds an M.A. and Ph.D. from Indiana University, Bloomington, in rhetoric, with a minor in Women's Studies. She began her career at IUPUI in 1993 and she became an adjunct professor of the Women's Studies Program (WOST) in 1996. Since 2012, she has been the Director of the Women's Studies Program, renamed Women's, Gender, and Sexuality Studies Program (WGSS) in 2018. She is the recipient of eight Teaching Excellence Recognition (TERA) Awards and is a member of the Faculty Colloquium for Excellence in Teaching (FACET) at IU. Her research focuses on the rhetoric of motherhood and intersections of race, class, culture, ethnicity, and gender. She has published in the *Howard Journal of Communications, The Southern Journal of Communication, GEMS, Women and Language*, and has contributed numerous chapters to textbooks on women and gender.

Mary E. King, PhD, is a professor in the Department of Communication Studies at Bloomsburg University. She is a proud mom to two little boys, Wesley (born August 2015) and William (born December 2017).

Dannabang Kuwabong, PhD, is a professor of postcolonial Caribbean literature in English at the University of Puerto Rico, Rio Piedras Campus. He has published widely in different fields in academic journals and contributed numerous essays in books and journals. His books include *Voices from Kibuli Country* and *Caribbean Blues & Love's Genealogy*. He has coauthored and coedited books, including *Myth Performance in African Diaspora Drama: Ritual, Theatre, and Dance*, as well as *Mothers and Daughters*. His critical essays on the Caribbean and Caribbean-Canadian literature and mothering have appeared in *Journal of the Motherhood Initiative (Journal for the Association of Research on Mothering)*; *From Motherhood to Mothering: The Legacy of Adrienne Rich's Of Woman Born*; *Confluences I & II: Essays in the New Canadian Literature*; *Creative Contradictions; Positive Interferences; Caribbean Studies; Sargasso*; and *Kola Magazine*.

Silvia Rivera Largacha, PhD, is an assistant professor at the School of Medicine and Health Sciences, Rosario University (Bogota-Colombia). Using conceptual tools from psychology, psychoanalysis, and cultural studies, her research explores the social construction of the body in different contemporary scenarios: drug consumption, body modification, and the experience of pregnancy, birth, and motherhood. Dr. Rivera's most recent publication is a chapter in the volume *Psychoanalysis and Criminology Today* (Presses Universitaires de Rennes).

Zsuzsanna Lénárt-Muszka, PhD, an instructor at the North American Department of the Institute of English and American Studies, University of Debrecen, Hungary. The title of her dissertation is *Mothers in the Wake of Slavery: The Im/possibility of Motherhood in Post-1980 African American Women's Prose* (2021). Her research interests include the portrayals of maternal bodies and subjectivities in contemporary American literature and visual culture, Black feminism, girlhood studies, Afropessimism, and Canadian literature.

Janice Tuck Lively, PhD, is a fiction writer and a professor of creative writing and literature at Elmhurst University. Her fiction and nonfiction celebrate and examine the joys and struggles of Black women's lives and have appeared in the journals *Jet Fuel Review, Perspectives on African American Literature, Journal of Black Studies, Valley Voices: A Literary Review,* and *Obsidian III: Literature in the African Diaspora*; and in the anthologies, *The Thing About Love Is...* and *Hair Trigger: 16.*

Catherine Ma, PhD, (she/her/hers) is an associate professor of psychology at The City University of New York (CUNY). She earned her PhD in social-personality psychology from the Graduate Center, CUNY, and is a mother to three fabulous children who make her proud every day. She immigrated to the United States from Kowloon, Hong Kong, became a naturalized citizen at the age of eight, and overcame many struggles as a first-generation college student. She has presented and written extensively on the maternal experiences of breastfeeding, mothering challenges in medicine, critiquing the current breastfeeding paradigm, racial bias in youth sports, the impact of Asian American studies in academia, imposter syndrome, and antiracism pedagogy in the classroom. Her love of research parallels her love of teaching at a racially diverse college because she finds it a privilege to teach students who share similar beginnings. Dr. Ma is an active board member of the Asian American/Asian Research Institute of CUNY and dedicates her time to mentoring students of colour. She established the Yuet Chun & Tai Yee Ma Memorial Endowed Scholarship Fund to honour the legacy of her grandparents.

Jessica A. Pauly, PhD, is an assistant professor in the Department of Communication at Utah Valley University. She gave birth to her first child, a girl, in January 2017.

Heather Robinson, PhD, is a Professor of English at York College-CUNY. Her research explores feminist issues in academic administration and the translingual languaging practices of multilingual tertiary students and urban communities. Her coauthored book, *Translingual Identities and Translingual Realities in the U.S. College Classroom*, was published by Routledge Press (2020), and she has also written articles and book chapters that appear in *Journal of Basic Writing*, *Administrative Theory and Praxis*, and *Teaching American Speech*. She also has two daughters doing virtual elementary school in the pandemic, and that is taking up a lot of mothering time.

Sherean Shehada is a doctoral student in Literatures of the Caribbean in English at the University of Puerto Rico, Río Piedras. Her work has appeared in *Positive Interferences: Unsettling Resonances in the Study of the Languages, Literatures, and Cultures of the Greater Caribbean and Beyond* (2019). She also participated in international seminars, such GUSEGG —Graz International Summer School Seggau, University of Graz, Austria. A soccer mom, she spends her non-academic time tending to her two boys, Mohammad & Saeed.

Dorsía Smith Silva, PhD, is a full professor of English at the University of Puerto Rico, Río Piedras. Her poetry has been published in several journals, including *Portland Review*, *Storyscape*, *Pigeonholes*, *Mom*

Egg Review, and *Moko Magazine.* Her articles have been widely published as well, including the *Journal of Caribbean Literature.* She is also the editor of *Latina/Chicana Mothering* and the coeditor of six books.

Meredith Stephens is on the faculty in the Department of International Liberal Arts, Institute of Socio-Arts and Sciences, Tokushima University, Japan. She graduated in Japanese and Linguistics from Adelaide University and obtained a Master of Arts in Applied Linguistics from Macquarie University. Her research interests include English language pedagogy in Japan and expatriate motherhood in Japan.

Hannah Swamidoss, PhD., received her doctoral degree in Literary Studies at The University of Texas at Dallas, specializing in British and American fiction, postcolonial theory, and children's literature. Dr. Swamidoss taught Education Management at Garland ISD (Sachse High School) in Texas until her passing. She published several articles in peer-reviewed academic journals and four book chapters, with three other book chapters in the process of being published.

Mary Barbara Walsh, PhD, is a professor of political science at Elmhurst University. She teaches courses on ancient, modern, and postmodern political philosophy, early American political thought, feminist political philosophy, and political justice. Her research focuses on liberal and feminist political philosophy and has been published in numerous journals, including *Hypatia, Review of Politics, Polity,* and *Journal of Women, Politics, and Policy.*

Nicole Willey, PhD, is a professor of English at Kent State University Tuscarawas, where she teaches a variety of literature and writing courses and serves as mentoring program coordinator for KSU Tuscarawas. Her research interests include mothering, masculinities, memoir, pedagogy, mentoring, nineteenth-century American literature, and slave narratives. She authored *Creating a New Ideal of Masculinity for American Men: The Achievement of Sentimental Women Writers in the Mid-Nineteenth Century* and coedited the collections *Motherhood Memoirs: Mothers Creating/Writing Lives* and *Feminist Fathering/Fathering Feminists: New Definitions and Directions.* She lives in New Philadelphia, Ohio, with her husband and two sons.

Deepest appreciation to
Demeter's monthly Donors

DEMETER

Daughters
Rebecca Bromwich
Summer Cunningham
Tatjana Takseva
Debbie Byrd
Fiona Green
Tanya Cassidy
Vicki Noble
Bridget Boland
Naomi McPherson
Myrel Chernick

Sisters
Amber Kinser
Nicole Willey
Christine Peets